Steck-Vaughn
Think-Alongs™
Comprehending As You Read
Level B

Teacher's Edition

Program Authors

Senior Author
Roger Farr

Co-Authors
Jennifer Conner
Elizabeth Haydel
Bruce Tone
Beth Greene
Tanja Bisesi
Cheryl Gilliland

STECK-VAUGHN
ELEMENTARY · SECONDARY · ADULT · LIBRARY

A Harcourt Company

www.steck-vaughn.com

Acknowledgments

Editorial Director	Diane Schnell
Project Editor	Anne Souby
Associate Director of Design	Cynthia Ellis
Design Manager	Ted Krause
Production and Design	Julia Miracle-Hagaman
Photo Editor	Claudette Landry
Product Manager	Patricia Colacino
Cover Design	Ted Krause
Cover Sculpture	Lonnie Springer
Cover Production	Alan Klemp

Think-Alongs™ is a trademark of Steck-Vaughn Company.

ISBN 0-7398-0090-6

Contents

We have all had the experience of reading a page and then not remembering what we read. For those of us who are good readers, this experience only occurs once in a while, when we are distracted and thinking about something else. But for newer readers or poor readers, this experience occurs repeatedly. They read the words on the page without making connections or visualizing what they are reading. They *are* reading, but they are not comprehending. For these students, and for all of us at times, it can be too easy to read the words on the page without thinking about the meaning of those words.

How can you encourage students to think while they read?

The **Steck-Vaughn Think-Alongs™: Comprehending As You Read** series is designed to provide you with a tool to do just that. In this series, students will learn to engage in a process called "thinking along." Whether students are thinking aloud or responding to written questions, the activities in this series will help them think as they read. By practicing the strategies presented here, students will become better comprehenders of the variety of texts they will encounter in school, in testing situations, and in their personal lives. These reading comprehension and critical thinking strategies will help students understand all texts, both expository and narrative, and help them feel successful about reading.

The **Steck-Vaughn Think-Alongs: Comprehending As You Read** series is designed to provide opportunities for students to:

- Think and comprehend as they read.
- Learn the reading strategies needed to become more effective comprehenders.
- Practice effective reading strategies with a variety of texts.
- Construct meaning as they read.
- Become more effective in their use of metacognitive reading strategies.
- Connect what they know to what is being read.
- Develop techniques that promote more effective reading.
- Write while reading, thus encouraging them to think about the text.
- Discuss the story and internalize unfamiliar vocabulary.
- Learn to use ideas developed while reading to write more effectively.
- Practice thinking strategies that can be used to improve reading comprehension test-taking skills.

The activities in this book are designed to work with your classroom goals and schedule. The activities are flexible and can be adjusted to suit your students' needs and your personal teaching style. The program provides a way for you to model the think-along process for students by using the "Introducing Thinking Along" section on pages T12–T15. The student books are easy to use, and the teacher's edition provides numerous activities for introducing, discussing, and extending each of the selections.

About the Author

Dr. Roger Farr, program author of **Steck-Vaughn Think-Alongs: Comprehending As You Read**, has been working on the strategies in this program for more than a decade. He has conducted hundreds of workshops and seminars with teachers over the years, has been directly involved with students in applying these strategies, and has received feedback from many teachers who have used the techniques in their classrooms. Dr. Farr has applied this research to **Think-Alongs**, thus developing effective and easy-to-use strategies for both teaching and learning reading comprehension.

A teacher of kindergarten through graduate school, Dr. Farr is a senior author of *Signatures* and *Collections*, both K–6 reading programs from Harcourt School Publishers, and he also serves as a special consultant to Harcourt on assessment and measurement. He is Chancellors' Professor of Education and Director of the Center for Innovation in Assessment at Indiana University.

Dr. Farr is a former president of the International Reading Association. In 1984, the IRA honored Dr. Farr for outstanding lifetime contributions to the teaching of reading. In the same year, he was elected to the IRA Reading Hall of Fame, and in 1988 he was selected by the IRA as the Outstanding Reading Teacher Educator.

Components

The series consists of six pupil's editions for grades one through six and six accompanying annotated teacher's editions, as well as a video simulating actual classroom use.

Pupil's Editions

The pupil's editions are divided into four units in Levels A–C and three units in Levels D–F. Each unit of three selections introduces and then provides practice for a specific reading comprehension strategy. In the first selection, students answer questions related to that specific strategy as they read. In the second and third selections, students are asked strategy questions as well as an increasing number of open-ended questions. This scaffolding approach helps students apply various reading comprehension strategies as they read. The write-in boxes and the scaffolding approach provide structure and organization for students. The questions are different from many traditional reading questions in that there are no correct or incorrect responses. Students are encouraged to think about the text in their own way.

In addition, the pupil's editions include two sections that allow students to apply the think-along process to test-taking situations. These sections consist of three reading passages including think-along questions followed by multiple-choice and short-answer questions modeled after standardized tests. A purpose-setting question leads students to focus. These practice sections help improve students' test-taking skills.

Pupil's Edition Features

Strategies for thinking along are introduced and modeled. Students are given ample practice thinking along with real literature and then responding in writing.

The pupil's edition includes:

- *Introduction to the Strategy*
- *Reading Selection with Write-in Boxes*
- *Writing Activity*
- *Test-Taking Practice*

Introduction to the Strategy

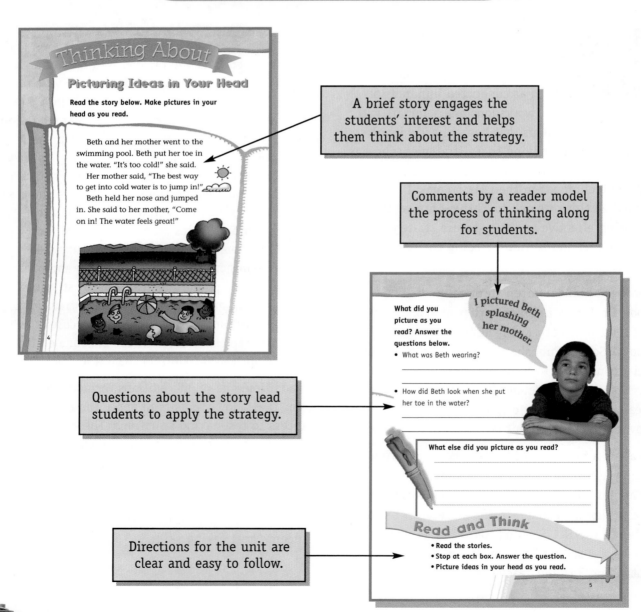

A brief story engages the students' interest and helps them think about the strategy.

Comments by a reader model the process of thinking along for students.

Questions about the story lead students to apply the strategy.

Directions for the unit are clear and easy to follow.

Thinking About

Picturing Ideas in Your Head

Read the story below. Make pictures in your head as you read.

Beth and her mother went to the swimming pool. Beth put her toe in the water. "It's too cold!" she said.

Her mother said, "The best way to get into cold water is to jump in!"

Beth held her nose and jumped in. She said to her mother, "Come on in! The water feels great!"

4

I pictured Beth splashing her mother.

What did you picture as you read? Answer the questions below.

- What was Beth wearing?

_____

- How did Beth look when she put her toe in the water?

What else did you picture as you read?

_____

Read and Think

- Read the stories.
- Stop at each box. Answer the question.
- Picture ideas in your head as you read.

5

Reading Selection

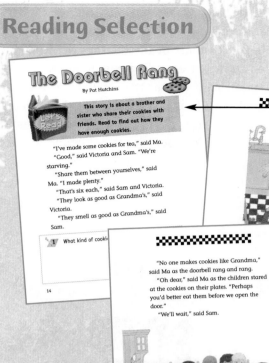

The Doorbell Rang
By Pat Hutchins

This story is about a brother and sister who share their cookies with friends. Read to find out how they have enough cookies.

"I've made some cookies for tea," said Ma.

"Good," said Victoria and Sam. "We're starving."

"Share them between yourselves," said Ma. "I made plenty."

"That's six each," said Sam and Victoria.

"They look as good as Grandma's," said Victoria.

"They smell as good as Grandma's," said Sam.

What kind of cooki...

14

"No one makes cookies like Grandma," said Ma as the doorbell rang and rang.

"Oh dear," said Ma as the children stared at the cookies on their plates. "Perhaps you'd better eat them before we open the door."

"We'll wait," said Sam.

...okies like Grandma,"
...ll rang.
...n with their four

...about now?

17

The **Let's Read** section introduces the selection and sets the purpose for reading.

Questions in the boxes throughout the selections encourage students to take "think breaks" as they read. These questions reinforce the strategies.

Full-color art or photos support the text and draw the reader into the text.

Writing Activity

Time to Write!

Grandma was good at making cookies. What is something that you do well?
• You will write a journal entry about something you do well.

Prewriting

First, make a list of three things you do well. Then decide which one of the three you enjoy the most and why.

1. I am good at _____ .
2. I am good at _____ .
3. I am good at _____ .

Which of these do you enjoy the most?

_____

I enjoy this the most because _____

...other sheet of paper
...ournal entry.

21

The **Time to Write!** page provides a writing prompt as well as a prewriting activity for a variety of writing experiences, including letters, reports, journal entries, and stories.

Test-Taking Practice

Thinking Along on Tests

• Read each story.
• Stop at each box. Answer the question.
• Answer the questions at the end of each story.

What does Grace get for her birthday?

"Happy birthday, Grace!" her brother Adam yelled. "Dad is bringing your present home with him! It's a pet! And it begins with the same letter as your name, g."

"Oh!" Grace cried. "What is it?"

What are you thinking about now?

HAPPY BIRTHDAY

56

Darken the circle for the correct answer.

1. Dad is bringing home a
Ⓐ bicycle
Ⓑ name
Ⓒ pet
Ⓓ picture

2. Who is having a birthday?
Ⓐ Adam
Ⓑ Grace
Ⓒ Dad
Ⓓ Mom

3. What letter is most important in this story?
Ⓐ h
Ⓑ b
Ⓒ s
Ⓓ g

4. Dad's gift was a _____ .
Ⓐ gorilla
Ⓑ giraffe
Ⓒ goat
Ⓓ goldfish

Write your answer on the lines below.
5. How does Adam feel at the beginning of the story?

_____

58

Test-taking practice sections help students apply the think-along concept to standardized test-taking situations.

Students are given both multiple-choice and short-answer questions as standardized test-taking practice.

Teacher's Edition

The teacher's edition provides suggestions for introducing each strategy as well as a lesson plan for each selection. The teacher's edition also includes reduced pupil pages with possible student responses and suggestions for how to interpret and react to those responses. These suggestions indicate the strategies that the student responses reflect.

Highlighted throughout the teacher's edition are three types of additional activities:

- **ESOL** activities include suggestions for helping students whose first language is not English apply the think-along strategies.
- **Meeting Individual Needs** activities address the needs of students with different learning styles.
- **Reinforcing the Strategies** helps students maintain previously learned strategies.

In addition, pages T12–T15 of the teacher's edition include directions for how to model the think-along process by thinking aloud so students can think along. Part of this demonstration includes coached practice for students.

Blackline Masters

The teacher's edition contains several blackline masters:

- Three stories to use with the optional teacher modeling section. (Note: When duplicating these masters for classroom use, adjust the setting on the photocopy machine so that the suggestions for teacher-directed questions in color will not reproduce on the student pages. Or, you may cover up these suggestions with a strip of paper when you photocopy these pages so they will not reproduce.)

- A letter to parents or caregivers in both English and Spanish to inform them of the program and provide suggestions for interacting with their children to increase reading comprehension.
- A self-assessment master that students can complete after they finish each selection. This evaluative tool helps students focus on metacognition and their attitudes about the think-along process.
- A scoring rubric for you to track students' progress in thinking along.

Video

A video accompanying the program features an introduction to the think-along process by Roger Farr and shows the program in use in actual classroom settings at several grade levels. It serves as a staff development tool for inservice or training purposes.

Teacher's Edition Features

The teacher's edition provides a wealth of information to enhance students' interaction with text through reading, writing, and discussion. At a glance, teachers can see a reduced pupil page. The program allows minimal preparation time and offers suggestions for maximizing instruction.

The teacher's edition features:

- Before Reading Activities
- Possible Responses
- Helpful Tips
- After Reading Activities

Before reading activities include:
- a clearly stated strategy,
- a summary of the selection for quick reference,
- a vocabulary list of unfamiliar words or words critical to understanding,
- suggestions for introducing the selection, and
- the purpose for reading.

Possible student responses demonstrate what to watch for and how to determine which strategies are being used. Questions are provided to further enhance student learning.

Helpful suggestions for meeting the individual needs of students, including those whose first language is not English, are given throughout the selections.

After reading activities include:
- suggestions for leading a discussion of what students write in the boxes. Such a discussion is a critical step in the think-along process.
- suggestions for reteaching the strategy to give additional options for student learning.

Each selection includes a list of additional activities and books on the topic to provide resources for further student interaction.

The writing section identifies ways for students to share what they have written.

Research Supporting Think-Along Strategies

Research during the past several decades has demonstrated that when students interact with text while reading, reading comprehension has improved. The impact of response techniques has been demonstrated in research involving reciprocal teaching, comprehension monitoring, think-aloud strategies, and writing in response to reading.

Do oral and written think-along activities help students understand what they are reading?

Ample research evidence demonstrates that active reasoning while reading enhances reading comprehension. Research has demonstrated the positive effects on reading comprehension when teachers ask thought-provoking questions while students are learning to read and when reading increasingly difficult new texts. Finally, numerous studies have demonstrated that good readers are active thinkers while reading.

Davey, Beth. **Think aloud—modeling the cognitive process of reading comprehension.** *Journal of Reading*, 27 (1), October 1983, pp. 44-47.

Kucan, Linda and Isabel L. Beck. **Four fourth graders thinking aloud: an investigation of genre effects**, *Journal of Literacy Research*, 28 (2), June 1996, pp. 259-287.

Loxterman, Jane. A, Isabel L. Beck, and Margaret G. McKeown. **The effects of thinking aloud during reading on students' comprehension of more or less coherent text.** *Reading Research Quarterly*, 29 (4), October-December 1994, pp. 352-367.

Pressley, Michael and Peter Afflerbach. **Verbal Protocols of Reading: The Nature of Constructively Responsive Reading.** Hillsdale, NJ: Lawrence Erlbaum Associates, 1995.

Does verbal or written interaction before and after reading enhance a reader's comprehension?

The research literature has documented the importance of a reader's active interaction with text—not only during reading, but also before and after reading. Readers who read with a purpose and discuss, write, and draw in active response to text are significantly better comprehenders than those who are passive readers.

McMahon, Susan I. and Taffy E. Raphael. **The Book Club Connection.** New York: Teachers' College Press, 1997.

Ogle, Donna. **Developing problem solving through language arts instruction.** In Collins, Cathy and John N. Mangieri (Eds.) *Teaching Thinking: An Agenda for the Twenty-First Century*. Hillsdale, NJ: Lawrence Erlbaum Associates, 1992, pp. 25-39.

Palincsar, Annemarie Sullivan and Ann L. Brown. **Reciprocal teaching of comprehension—fostering and comprehension monitoring activities.** *Cognition and Instruction*, 1 (2), 1984, pp. 117-125.

Does being aware of reading strategies help a reader comprehend more effectively and easily?

Awareness of reading strategies and how one is comprehending is called metacognition. The research on the positive impact of metacognitive strategies on reading comprehension is well documented.

Baker, Linda and Ann L. Brown. **Metacognitive skills and reading.** In Pearson, David P. (Ed.) *Handbook of Reading Research*. New York: Longman, 1984, pp. 353-394.

Farr, Roger, et al. **Writing in response to reading.** *Educational Leadership*, 47 (6), March 1990, pp. 66-69.

Paris, Scott G., Barbara A. Wasik, and Gert Van der Westhuizen. **Meta-metacognition: a review of research on metacognition and reading.** In Readence, John E. et al. (Eds.) *Dialogues in Literacy Research: Thirty-seventh Yearbook of The National Reading Conference*, National Reading Conference, 1988, pp. 143-166.

Raphael, Taffy E. and Clydie A. Wonnacott. **Heightening fourth-grade students' sensitivity to sources of information for answering comprehension questions.** *Reading Research Quarterly*, 20 (3), Spring 1985, pp. 282-296.

Tips for Using Think-Alongs in Your Classroom

An important aspect of using **Think-Alongs** in your classroom is to monitor and discuss students' responses to the questions in the boxes. The following tips will help you encourage and direct students in using **Think-Alongs**.

- Give positive feedback as you walk around the room and look at student responses.

- Check that students are responding to the questions in the boxes. If they cannot answer the question, have them write whatever they are thinking.

- If students are unable to write an answer to the question, encourage them to draw a picture. This is a particularly good strategy to use with students whose primary language is not English.

- Assure students that there are no wrong answers. Answers will vary because students are making their own connections with the text.

- Encourage students to write their ideas in the boxes fairly quickly and then continue reading the selection.

- The amount students write is not important. They do not have to write complete sentences.

- Spelling, grammar, and punctuation are not as important as thinking and responding.

- Students may use a variety of strategies as they respond to questions.

- If students write answers that are not clearly related to the selection, follow up by asking them why they wrote what they did.

- If students do not understand the meaning of a word, have them figure it out from the context, or have them keep a list of words to look up. Provide help when needed.

- For a student who struggles with the process, model for that student at a specific place in the selection.

Scoring the Tests

Scoring the tests can tell you how well your students are learning to use the think-along strategies. For each test, score 1 point for each multiple-choice question correct (total 12) and 2 points for each open-ended response (total 6). Add the two for a total of up to 18 points for the test. Refer to the chart below for how to interpret the raw score.

Interpreting Test Scores

Raw Score	Letter Grade	Number Grade
16–18	A	90–100
13–15	B	80–89
10–12	C	70–79
Below 10	D	Below 70

Planning Further Instruction

Scores of 90 or above are excellent. These students are good readers and should be encouraged to continue independent reading. The students are probably thinking extensively while they read. Occasional practice in the think-along strategies, especially as new content area materials and new genres are introduced, would be worthwhile.

Scores of 70 to 90 fall in a range of good to satisfactory. These students need to continue to write what they are thinking as they read. Discussing with students what they have written will be helpful to strengthen their comprehending strategies. These students will also profit from the introduction of these strategies with different reading genres and content areas.

Scores below 70 are unsatisfactory. It would be useful for these students to work in small groups with you using the suggestions on pages T12–T15. Teacher modeling as well as encouraging student oral and written responses will help these students use reading strategies more effectively.

Introducing Thinking Along

The following warm-up activities are optional. Feel free to modify the activities to meet your teaching goals and students' needs. These activities introduce your students to what it means to think along while reading. These activities will be valuable for all of your students, but especially for those who have difficulties comprehending what they read.

Activity 1
Modeling

Think aloud so your students can think along!

Read the Story Aloud

"Each owner thought his or her dog was the best."

First, model thinking along with your students by thinking aloud while you read. Use the story "The Dog Show" (Master 1 on pages T16–T19). Duplicate enough copies so that each student has one. Throughout the story you will find suggestions of what to say at certain points in the text. (Note: When duplicating these masters for classroom use, adjust the setting on the photocopy machine so that the text in color will not reproduce on the student pages. Or, you may cover up the text in color with a strip of paper so they will not reproduce on the student pages.)

I know how they feel. I would want my dog to win, too, because I think she is the best.

Activity 2
Providing Coached Practice

Get students to think along by asking specific questions.

Next, have students start thinking along with a story. Read the story "Wish on a Star" (Master 2 on pages T20–T23) aloud to students. You may duplicate copies for your students.

Again, photocopy the pages so that the type in color does not reproduce on the student pages. Stop at the points marked in the story and call on individual students to answer the questions provided in the text.

Read the Story Aloud

"'Just look at all of the stars out tonight!' Mama said."

Have you ever looked at the stars on a clear night?

Yes, I like looking for the Big Dipper.

TIPS

In "Wish on a Star" places are marked to ask questions to elicit these strategies:

- Prediction
- Personal Experience
- Visualization

Activity 3
Providing More Coached Practice

Get students to think along by asking, "What are you thinking about now?"

Next, have students think along by asking them the more general question, "What are you thinking about now?" Read the story "Who's That Knocking?" (Master 3 on pages T24–T28) aloud to students.

You may duplicate copies for your students. (Photocopy the pages so the type in color does not reproduce.) Stop at the points marked in the story and call on individual students to answer the questions provided in the text.

Read the Story Aloud

"'Maybe Melissa is playing games with us,' April said."

What are you thinking about now?

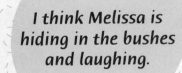
I think Melissa is hiding in the bushes and laughing.

TIPS

- If a student has trouble answering the general "What are you thinking about now" question, ask a more specific question, such as "What might happen next?"

- Have several students tell you what they are thinking about each time you stop.

- After a few students have shared their thoughts, share your own as well.

T14

Activity 4
Reflecting

Get students to reflect on their responses and on the process of thinking along.

Next, have students think about their responses to the questions and how they feel about the process of thinking along. Respond to students' answers in a positive way, but if their answers seem unrelated to the reading, ask for clarification. Point out the strategies they are using. Note the individual approaches they are taking to show that many different answers are acceptable.

Finally, ask students how they feel about using the think-along process.

What do you think about the think-along process?

Thinking along is fun. It makes me think of things I don't usually think about when I read stories.

TIPS

To get students to support their responses:

- "That's an interesting idea. What made you think of that?"
- "I think I know what you mean. Can you explain a little more?"
- "I never thought of that. What made you think of that?"
- "I like that idea. Where did it come from?"

To get students to diversify their responses:

- "What an interesting idea! No one else thought of that."
- "Who else has another way of thinking about the story?"

To get students to use different strategies:

- "What do you think will happen next?"
- "What does the story remind you of?"
- "What picture does this make in your mind?"

The Dog Show

"Let's have a dog show," Amanda said. "I saw one on TV. They look like a lot of fun."

"Almost everyone on the block has a dog," Jamal said. He was excited about the idea. "This will be fun!"

They talked to their friend Luis. He did not have a dog, but he thought it would be fun to have a dog show. He said he would help make posters.

Dog shows are interesting. I went to a dog show once and liked seeing so many different kinds of dogs.

I think it's great that people without dogs want to take part in the dog show. I think that will make it more fun for everyone.

"We are going to need a prize," Amanda said.

"I'll ask my dad to give some dog toys from his pet store," Jamal said. ....▶ I wonder what kind of toys his dad will bring. I think he might bring bones, squeaky toys, and a tug rope.

"Who will be the judge?" Luis asked.

"My dad knows a lot about dogs," Jamal said. "I'll ask him to be the judge."

Jamal's dad said he would be the judge and promised to bring the prizes. ....▶ I wonder how Jamal's dad will decide which dog should win.

There were eleven dogs in the show. Each owner thought his or her dog was the best. ....

> I know how they feel. I would want my dog to win, too, because I think she is the best.

When it came time to name the winner, Jamal's dad held up a rubber bone and said, "Amanda's dog wins for wagging its tail best!" Everyone looked surprised. ....

> I think that's a funny reason to choose the winning dog! I think it's nice to give a prize to the dog that wags its tail the best, because that means it is very happy.

Then Jamal's dad began handing out other prizes. There was one for a dog in a funny hat. There was one for a dog that shook hands and another for a dog that could "speak" in barks.

In the end, every dog at the show got a prize. Everyone was happy. Each dog was the best. ....▶ I like picturing each of these dogs doing something special. I think it's great that every dog got a prize for being itself.

Wish on a Star

It was a very clear night. The family sat on the front steps talking about the summer.

"Just look at all of the stars out tonight!" Mama said. ....▶ Have you ever looked at the stars on a clear night?

"They're beautiful!" Cecilia sighed. She loved these summer nights with her family.

"It is a very nice night," Papa said. "It is not as hot as it was last night." ....▶ What do you think about when you look at the stars?

"I love the stars," Cecilia whispered. "Oh, look! A shooting star! Did you know that you can wish on a shooting star?" she asked.

▶ What do you picture a shooting star looks like?

"Make a wish, then," Mama said.

"I wish that all our nights would not be too hot. Just like this one," Cecilia said.

Her sister Teresa frowned. "That won't come true," she sighed.

"I wish that we will go on a trip to Mexico this summer," Cecilia said.

"That is your second wish," Papa said. "Do you get more than one?"

▶ Do you think Cecilia will make more wishes?

"I have seen a lot of shooting stars tonight," Cecilia said. "I wish that summer would last forever."

Why do you think that Cecilia wishes that summer would last forever?

Teresa groaned. "That would be great," she said. "But winter will come whether we like it or not."

"Okay, then, I wish my best friend would move in next door to us," Cecilia said.

"I don't think that wish is going to come true either, Cecilia," said Teresa.

"Well, then," Cecilia said, "I give up."

What do you think will happen next?

"Why don't you try a wish, Teresa?" Mama asked.

"I already did," Teresa said. "And it has come true!" ....

"What do you think that Teresa wished for?"

Cecilia was excited to hear that. "What did you wish, Teresa?" she cried.

"I wished that we could stay up late and look at the stars!" Teresa said. ....

"What would you wish for if you saw a shooting star?"

Who's That Knocking?

"Ratta, tat, tat . . . tap, tap, tap."

"Somebody is at the back door," Keisha said.

"Who could it be?" April wondered.

The girls sat silently, listening for it again.

"Ratta, tat, tat . . . tap, tap, tap."

"It sounds like somebody wants in," Keisha said.

"We can't let anyone in," April said. "We're not supposed to answer the door for strangers."

"It's probably Melissa," Keisha said. "She said she might be able to play with us today."

What are you thinking about now?

"Tap . . . tap . . . tap!" The knocking sounded louder this time.

The girls went to the kitchen and peeked out the window. There was no one on the porch in back. ....

► What are you thinking about now?

"It's not Melissa," Keisha said. "I wonder who it was." The girls returned to the pictures they were making.

April pointed at Keisha's drawing. "What is that?" she asked.

"It's a mystery," Keisha said. She held her drawing up like a picture on a wall.

"Ratta, tat, tat . . . tap, tap, tap."

The girls sat up straight.

Then Keisha ran to the kitchen window again. "There's no one out there," she said.

"Maybe Melissa is playing games with us," April said.

Slowly April opened the back door and peeked out. Keisha was right. There was no one out there. "Talk about a mystery!" April said.

▶ What are you thinking about now?

"Melissa?" Keisha called out.

No one answered.

The girls returned to their pictures. But Keisha kept looking back over her shoulder at the door.

Soon they heard it again. It was not as loud this time.

Quickly April ran to the door and opened it.

The porch was empty!

▶What are you thinking about now?

Keisha looked out and down along the back of the house.

"Look!" she said.

April looked and saw a little patch of black and white and red.

It was a red-headed woodpecker!

It was pounding its beak against a windowsill. Then it flew out to a birdbath in the yard. It sat turning its head and looking at the girls. ....

▶ What are you thinking about now?

"You can stop knocking, bird!" April giggled. "You can't come in."

At Home

Dear family of _____ ,

Our class has begun to read stories and articles in a book titled **Steck-Vaughn Think-Alongs™: Comprehending As You Read.** The book uses an approach to reading called "thinking along." Your child will be answering questions as he or she reads, not waiting until the end of the selection to answer questions. In this way, your child will understand and remember better what he or she has read.

You can help your child in many ways. Ask your child about the readings and about the reading strategies he or she is studying in class. Ask how your child feels about thinking along while reading. Read with your child, stopping as you read to discuss the story, such as what has happened and what might happen next.

Encourage your child to think as he or she reads. You will find that he or she will

- comprehend what he or she reads,

- remember it better, and

- enjoy reading more.

Sincerely,

En la casa

Estimada familia de _____,

Nuestra clase ha comenzado a leer cuentos y artículos de un libro titulado **Steck-Vaughn Think-Alongs™: Comprehending As You Read.** El libro utiliza un enfoque a la lectura llamado "thinking along" (pensar mientras lee). Su niño/a contestará preguntas mientras él o ella lea, sin esperar hasta el final de la selección para responder a las preguntas. En esta forma, su niño/a comprenderá y recordará mejor lo que él o ella haya leído.

Usted puede ayudar a su niño/a de muchas maneras. Hágale preguntas sobre las lecturas y acerca de las destrezas que está aprendiendo en la clase. Pregúntele cómo se siente mientras piensa cuando está leyendo. Lea con su niño/a, deteniéndose mientras leen para comentar el cuento, y conversar acerca de lo que ha ocurrido y de lo ocurrirá después.

Anime a su niño/a a pensar sobre lo que lee. Usted se dará cuenta de que él o ella

- comprenderá lo que está leyendo,
- recordará mejor lo que ha leído, y
- disfrutará más de la lectura.

Atentamente,

Thinking About Thinking Along

Read each statement below. Mark the answer that tells how you feel about thinking along as you read.

1. I can write in the boxes when I read.

True for me.   **Not true for me.**   **I'm not sure.**

2. Writing in the boxes helps me understand what I read.

True for me.   **Not true for me.**   **I'm not sure.**

3. Writing in the boxes helps me remember what I read.

True for me.   **Not true for me.**   **I'm not sure.**

4. Writing in the boxes helps me discuss what I read with others.

True for me.   **Not true for me.**   **I'm not sure.**

Read and answer the question below.

5. Which selection was the most fun to think about when you wrote in the boxes? Why?

_____

_____

_____

_____

_____

_____

Student _____ Date _____

Checklist for Assessing Thinking Along

RATING				
Not at all				All the time
1	2	3	4	5

How is thinking along working with this student?

1. Is the student able to write in the boxes?   1   2   3   4   5

2. Does the student discuss what he or she wrote   1   2   3   4   5
in the boxes?

3. Can the student support and defend what he   1   2   3   4   5
or she wrote?

4. Does the student use a variety of reading   1   2   3   4   5
comprehension strategies?

5. Does the student seem to understand the   1   2   3   4   5
selection and remember what he or she reads?

6. Does the student pay more attention now to   1   2   3   4   5
the text when he or she reads?

7. Does the student apply thinking along   1   2   3   4   5
to other subjects?

8. Does the student ask more questions when   1   2   3   4   5
reading in other subject areas?

9. Does the student discuss more about what he   1   2   3   4   5
or she reads in other subject areas?

10. Does the student apply reading comprehension   1   2   3   4   5
strategies in other subject areas?

Scope and Sequence

Strategy	Level					
	A	B	C	D	E	F
Retell by drawing pictures	x	x	x	x	x	x
Connect personal experiences	x	x	x	x	x	x
Identify the main idea	x	x	x	x	x	x
Make predictions	x	x	x	x	x	x
Visualize		x	x	x	x	x
Generate questions		x	x	x	x	x
Identify main ideas and details		x	x	x	x	x
Recognize sequence		x	x	x	x	x
Use background knowledge			x	x	x	x
Compare and contrast			x	x	x	x
Make and revise predictions			x	x	x	x
Distinguish between fantasy and reality			x	x	x	x
Identify cause and effect				x	x	x
Summarize				x	x	x
Identify author's purpose				x	x	x
Draw conclusions					x	x
Evaluate and express opinions					x	x
Identify and interpret meaning of figurative language					x	x
Analyze story elements						x
Identify and analyze problems and solutions						x
Evaluate and interpret author's style and technique						x

Strategy Definitions

Level A

Retell by drawing pictures: Students listen to or read a story and then draw one or more pictures to retell the story.

Connect personal experiences: Students recognize similarities between themselves and their lives and the characters and events in the selections they listen to or read independently.

Identify the main idea: Students express the main idea of a selection either in words or in pictures.

Make predictions: Students speculate about what will happen next in a story.

Level B

Visualize: Students try to picture in their heads what they are reading or listening to in a selection.

Generate questions: Students question events, characters, and details as they read.

Identify main ideas and details: Students determine both explicit and implicit main ideas of a selection. They identify details that support the main idea.

Recognize sequence: Students recall events in a selection in the order in which they occur. They also predict what will happen next or what happened prior to the events described in the selection.

Level C

Use background knowledge: Students use what they already know to interpret the ideas in narrative and expository selections.

Compare and contrast: Students compare relationships between events, objects, or characters to see how they are alike and different.

Make and revise predictions: Students speculate about what will happen next in a narrative or expository selection. They confirm or change their predictions based on subsequent information.

Distinguish between fantasy and reality: Students recognize the difference between what could be real and what could not be real.

Level D

Identify cause and effect: Students identify why something happened (cause) and the consequence of an event or action (effect).

Summarize: Students use textual and typographical clues to recognize the organization of expository text. They use the text organization to summarize the selection.

Identify author's purpose: Students understand an author's purpose in writing a particular story or article. They also are able to identify writing for a specific purpose such as to inform, explain, or entertain.

Level E

Draw conclusions: Students use the information provided in a selection to form a conclusion or make inferences about the topic of the selection.

Evaluate and express opinion: Students develop opinions about the subject or content of a selection or evaluate the opinions expressed by the author or character in a selection.

Identify and interpret meaning of figurative language: Students recognize vivid and colorful language that helps to set the mood of a selection or conveys feelings. They interpret the meaning of figurative language.

Level F

Analyze story elements: Students identify and analyze the characters, setting, theme, or plot in a story.

Identify and analyze problems and solutions: Students identify a problem that is stated or implied in a selection and evaluate the solutions presented in the selection.

Evaluate and interpret author's style and technique: Students determine why an author may have written a selection and how the author's writing style and technique makes the selection interesting or unusual.

Annotated Student Pages for

Steck-Vaughn Think-Alongs:
Comprehending As You Read

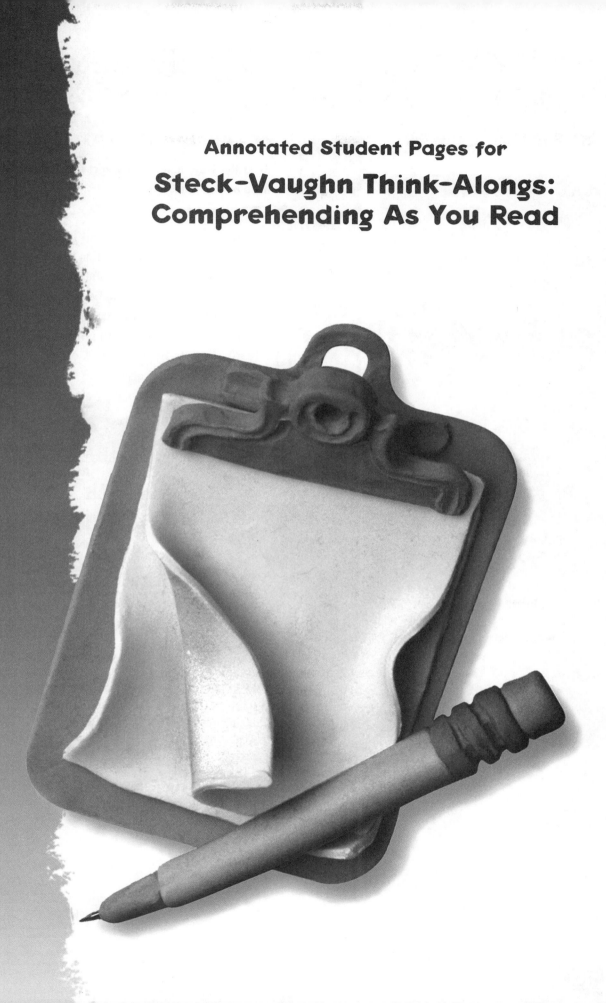

Thinking About...

Picturing Ideas in Your Head

Visualizing

Readers enhance their comprehension of a text when they picture what people, places, and events look like as they read. Even when illustrations accompany a text, good readers do not rely solely on what they see in the text. Good readers add details or even make adjustments to printed illustrations by forming visual representations in their minds.

Thinking About

Picturing Ideas in Your Head

Read the story below. Make pictures in your head as you read.

Beth and her mother went to the swimming pool. Beth put her toe in the water. "It's too cold!" she said.

Her mother said, "The best way to get into cold water is to jump in!"

Beth held her nose and jumped in. She said to her mother, "Come on in! The water feels great!"

4

Introducing the Strategy

Read aloud a section or page from a book to students without showing them the illustrations that accompany the text. Have students draw a picture illustrating what you read. After students have completed their drawings, have them share their pictures with one another. Show students the illustration from the book. Point out that everyone imagines characters, places, and events from a story in different ways.

Applying the Strategy

Ask students to follow along as you read the selection in the pupil book, or have a volunteer read it. Tell them to think about how Beth and her mother look in the story.

What did you picture as you read? Answer the questions below.

I pictured Beth splashing her mother.

- What was Beth wearing?

_____

_____

- How did Beth look when she put her toe in the water?

_____

_____

What else did you picture as you read?

_____

_____

_____

_____

Read and Think

- Read the stories.
- Stop at each box. Answer the question.
- Picture ideas in your head as you read.

5

Have students complete the visualization questions independently or as a group. Ask students what they were thinking about while the selection was read. Ask questions such as the following:
- *Why was Beth afraid to go into the swimming pool?*
- *What did you picture Beth wearing?*
- *What would you have done if you were Beth?*

Explain to students that they will be thinking about how people, places, and events look as they read the selections in this unit.

Read and Think

Read the directions so that students know what they are to do in the unit. Explain that they are to answer the questions in the boxes as they read the selections.
- Remind students that answering the questions in the boxes will help them think about the selections.
- Tell them that they can draw pictures to show what they are thinking.
- Encourage them to picture people, places, and events in their heads as they read the selections.

Strategy Focus

Visualizing to think about a selection.

Story at a Glance

A boy and his teacher do many of the same things while getting ready for the first day of school.

Vocabulary

You may want to introduce the following words to your students:
sardines
sneaker
briefcase
wondering

Getting Students Started

· *Introducing the Selection*

Ask students to talk about what they do and how they feel on the first day of school. Then share with students those things that *you* do that they also talked about doing. Tell students that you have a lot of the same feelings they talked about having on the first day of school.

· *Purpose for Reading*

Students read to find out what a boy and his teacher do while getting ready for the first day of school.

It Happens to Everyone

By Bernice Myers

This story is about a boy and his teacher getting ready for the first day of school. Read to find out what they do that is the same.

It's Monday morning. Michael is up early. He's very excited because today is the first day of school. Michael can't decide what clothes to wear.

6

Mrs. Daniel can't decide what to wear,
either. She's the new teacher, and it's the
first day of school for her, too.

Before breakfast Michael feeds his pets.

> **1** What pets do you picture Michael feeding?

Mrs. Daniel gives her cat some sardines.

7

Strategy Tip

Remind students that a story
might show its characters in
pictures, but sometimes there
are no pictures and they have
to imagine what those
people look like.

Possible Responses
Question 1

dogs cats fish
  Sometimes students will
respond to questions by
listing one-word ideas.
Encourage this student to
expand on his or her
response by asking, "What
kinds of food might you feed
these pets?"

I feed my hamsters.
  This student is drawing on
personal experience to help
make sense of the story. Ask,
"Do you think that Michael
might have a pet hamster?"

**I don't know. Mrs. Daniel has
a cat.**
  This student is having trouble picturing the type of pet
Michael might have. To help
this student visualize, ask,
"What kinds of pets do you,
or someone you know,
have?"

Michael is in a hurry to get to school.
He spills his milk and gets peanut butter
all over his sweater.

Mrs. Daniel is in a hurry, too. She spills
her coffee.

Michael can't find his other sneaker.
He looks at the clock. It's getting late.

Mrs. Daniel can't find her glasses. She
looks at her watch. It's already 8 o'clock.

8

Michael ties his sneaker, grabs his lunch, and runs out the door.

Mrs. Daniel grabs her bag and her briefcase and runs out the door.

The school bus stops in front of Michael's house. He gets there just in time.

 2 What do you picture is happening on the bus?

9

Possible Responses
Question 2

I think the children are talking to one another.

To emphasize that readers use personal experience when they visualize, ask this student, "Is that what you do when you ride the school bus?"

They might be looking at Michael because he just got on the bus.

This student is visualizing a probable scene on the school bus. Ask, "What else might the children be doing on the bus?"

He is nervous.

Although this student does not address the question, he or she is empathizing with the main character. Say, "You're thinking about how Michael feels. That's great. What are you picturing the children doing on the bus?"

Mrs. Daniel just misses her bus. She has to drive to school in her car.

Michael is a little nervous. He's wondering what school will be like.

Mrs. Daniel is a little nervous, too.

Michael goes into the Boys' Room for a minute. Mrs. Daniel goes into the Ladies' Room.

10

Michael bumps into a friend. Mrs. Daniel bumps into the principal.

 3 How do you think the principal looks?

Michael looks for his classroom. Mrs. Daniel looks for hers.

Michael hopes the new teacher likes him. Mrs. Daniel hopes her new students like her.

11

Meeting Individual Needs

For students who are having trouble writing responses in the boxes, have them draw their responses instead. Ask students to write brief captions that explain their drawings.

Possible Responses Question 3

Our principal is really tall.
This student is implicitly comparing and contrasting his or her own school principal with the principal in the story. To clarify, ask, "Are you picturing the principal in this story as being tall, too?"

He is wearing nice clothes.
This student is describing one aspect of the principal's appearance. Encourage the student to elaborate on this response by saying, "Tell me more about what the principal's clothes look like."

smart and nice
In this response, the student has described what the principal's personality might be like, but not what he or she might look like. Ask, "The principal might be smart and nice. What do you think the principal looks like?"

After Reading

It is very important to have students read and discuss what they pictured in their heads in response to the questions.

Discussing the Think-Alongs

- Give as many students as possible a chance to tell what they wrote in response to one of the questions.
- Have students explain what they were thinking when they wrote.
- Ask students how picturing what they are reading helps them think about the story.

Reteaching

For those students who have not written or are having difficulty with the activity:

- Ask them to tell you what they were thinking about as they read.
- Model your own use of visualization by sharing what you were picturing as you read.
- Ask questions that motivate students to picture what they are reading, such as the following:
  - *How fast did you picture Michael running to catch his bus?*
  - *What did you picture Mrs. Daniels doing after she bumped into the principal?*
  - *How many students did you picture in the classroom with Michael and Mrs. Daniels?*

Michael finds his room number. So does Mrs. Daniel! It's the same one as Michael's. They go inside together.

"Good morning, I'm Mrs. Daniel, and this is our first day in school together."

"I'm Michael!"   "I'm Mary!"   "I'm thirsty!"

4 What do you picture on the walls of Mrs. Daniel's classroom?

12

Possible Responses
Question 4

A picture of a dragon. Like the picture on Michael's wall at home.

This response demonstrates a strong critical reading of the story. The student understands that the story is about similarities between Michael and Mrs. Daniel, and has responded with these similarities in mind.

Maybe pictures.

Encourage this student to tell you more about the pictures he or she is visualizing by asking, "What do the pictures look like? Are they large or small?"

Nothing. It's the first day. No one has put things up yet.

This is an example of critical reading and thinking. To find out more about how the student arrived at his or her response, ask, "That's an interesting response. What made you think of that?"

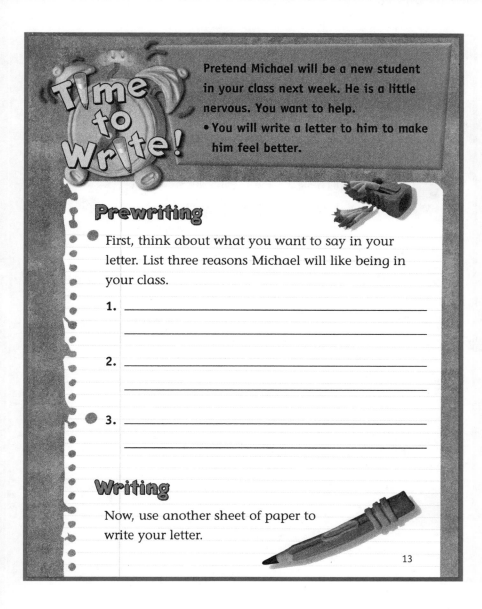

Time to Write!

Pretend Michael will be a new student in your class next week. He is a little nervous. You want to help.

• You will write a letter to him to make him feel better.

Prewriting

First, think about what you want to say in your letter. List three reasons Michael will like being in your class.

1. _____

_____

2. _____

_____

3. _____

_____

Writing

Now, use another sheet of paper to write your letter.

13

Prewriting

Explain that the prewriting activity will help students think of different reasons they enjoy being in their class.

Writing

Remind students that their letters should make Michael feel less nervous about coming to their class as a new student.

Sharing

Have students trade letters with a partner. Tell students to read their partner's letter as though they were Michael. Then, have students write a letter back to their partners, pretending that they are responding as Michael.

Making Connections

Activity Links

• Have students draw pictures of themselves welcoming Michael to their class.
• Ask students to think of words that describe themselves on the first day of school. Write the words on the board. Then have students choose one of the words on the board. Have them draw a picture of themselves that shows them feeling or acting in a way that represents the word they chose.
• Have students volunteer to act out the story.
• Ask students to make a list of school supplies they need for the first day of school and explain why each of these items is important.

Reading Links

You might want to include these books in a discussion of the first day of school:
• *Back to School for Rotten Ralph* by Jack Gantos (HarperCollins, 1998).
• *I'll Go to School If* by Bo Flood (Fairview Press, 1997).
• *Sparky and Eddie: First Day of School (Sparky and Eddie, No. 1)* by Tony Johnston (Scholastic Trade, 1997).

The Doorbell Rang

Strategy Focus

Visualizing to think about a selection.

Story at a Glance

Two children share cookies with their friends.

Vocabulary

You may want to introduce the following words to your students:
doorbell
share
cousins
enormous

Getting Students Started

- **Introducing the Selection**

  Ask students to talk about what they share with friends who come to their house. Tell students that they are going to read a story about two children who share cookies with their friends.

- **Purpose for Reading**

  Students read to find out how the children in the story keep from running out of cookies.

The Doorbell Rang

By Pat Hutchins

This story is about a brother and sister who share their cookies with friends. Read to find out how they have enough cookies.

"I've made some cookies for tea," said Ma.

"Good," said Victoria and Sam. "We're starving."

"Share them between yourselves," said Ma. "I made plenty."

"That's six each," said Sam and Victoria.

"They look as good as Grandma's," said Victoria.

"They smell as good as Grandma's," said Sam.

1 What kind of cookies do you picture?

14

Possible Responses
Question 1

oatmeal cookies
Encourage this student to elaborate on his or her response by asking, "How big are the oatmeal cookies you are picturing?"

There are 12 cookies.
Although this student has not responded to the question, his or her response indicates good comprehension of the text. Say, "Great, you were thinking about how many cookies there are. What kind of cookies are you picturing?"

My mom makes chocolate chip cookies. That's what I am picturing.
This student is not only visualizing the cookies but is also using personal experience to think about the text.

"No one makes cookies like Grandma," said Ma as the doorbell rang.

It was Tom and Hannah from next door.

"Come in," said Ma. "You can share the cookies."

"That's three each," said Sam and Victoria.

"They smell as good as your Grandma's," said Tom.

"And look as good," said Hannah.

Strategy Tip

Remind students that when they read, they should imagine how things in the story look. Sometimes the story includes pictures, but it helps for readers to fill in gaps on their own.

2 What else do you picture in the dining room?

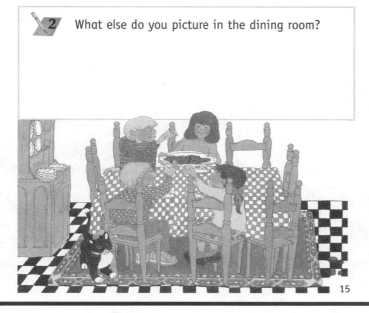

15

Possible Responses
Question 2

A dog. He wants a cookie.
This response indicates good comprehension of the story and use of personal experience and background knowledge. Ask, "What kind of dog are you picturing? What is the dog doing that makes you think he wants a cookie?"

There are always windows.
This student is using his or her background knowledge to help visualize what is in the dining room. Ask, "How big are the windows? What do you picture besides windows?"

chairs and pictures and candles
Encourage the student to describe the location of these items in the room by asking, "Where are the candles in the dining room? What kinds of pictures do you see?"

"No one makes cookies like Grandma," said Ma as the doorbell rang.

It was Peter and his little brother.

"Come in," said Ma.

"You can share the cookies."

"That's two each," said Victoria and Sam.

"They look as good as your Grandma's," said Peter.

"And smell as good."

16

"Nobody makes cookies like Grandma," said Ma as the doorbell rang.

It was Joy and Simon with their four cousins.

> **3** What are you thinking about now?

17

Possible Responses
Question 3

There are not enough cookies for everyone.

This student is making a prediction that reflects strong critical thinking skills. To encourage the student to elaborate on his or her prediction, ask, "What do you think they will do if they don't have enough cookies?"

The cousins.

Some students are uncomfortable expanding on information presented in a reading. They feel that if the information isn't in the text then it is not part of the story. Asking this student, "What are you thinking about the cousins?" is not likely to elicit a more thoughtful response. Instead, ask, "What color eyes do you think the cousins have?"

This story is making me hungry.

This student is reacting personally to the text, which shows good comprehension and strong interaction with the reading.

"Come in," said Ma. "You can share the cookies."

"That's one each," said Sam and Victoria.

"They smell as good as your Grandma's," said Joy.

"And look as good," said Simon.

"No one makes cookies like Grandma," said Ma as the doorbell rang and rang.

"Oh dear," said Ma as the children stared at the cookies on their plates. "Perhaps you'd better eat them before we open the door."

"We'll wait," said Sam.

19

As students read the story for the first time, have them re-read portions of the selection they do not understand. Re-reading portions of a selection as they go along will better support comprehension than waiting until the end to re-read the entire text. Ask students to write down unfamiliar words and help them define these words as they are reading.

It is very important to have students read and discuss what they wrote in response to the questions and to discuss what the questions encouraged them to visualize.

Discussing the Think-Alongs

- Give as many students as possible a chance to tell what they wrote in response to one of the questions.
- Have students explain what they were thinking when they wrote.
- Ask students how picturing what they read helps them think about the story.

Reteaching

For those students who have not written or are having difficulty with the activity:

- Ask students to draw pictures of each scene in the dining room where the cookies are being served and shared. Have them write captions for their drawings that describe who is in each picture.
- Model your own use of visualization by sharing what you were picturing as you read.
- Ask questions that motivate students to picture what they are reading, such as the following:
  - *How many cookies did you picture Grandma carrying when she walked through the door?*
  - *What kind of cookies did you picture Grandma carrying?*
  - *How did you picture Grandma?*

It was Grandma with an enormous tray of cookies.

"How nice to have so many friends to share them with," said Grandma. "It's a good thing I made a lot!"

"And no one makes cookies like Grandma," said Ma as the doorbell rang.

4 Who do you picture at the door now?

20

Possible Responses Question 4

maybe Grandpa
This student is using his or her background knowledge and personal experience to visualize who might be at the door. Ask, "What does Grandpa look like? Is he bringing anything for the children?"

a teacher
One of the reasons why it is important to have students explain their responses is because what may be obvious to the student is not always obvious to others. Ask, "Why do you think it might be a teacher? What does the teacher look like?"

probably more kids
This response indicates good comprehension. The student has recognized the pattern established in the story and has provided a response that follows the story pattern. Encourage the student to describe the kids by asking, "How many kids do you think might be at the door? How old are they? What do they look like?"

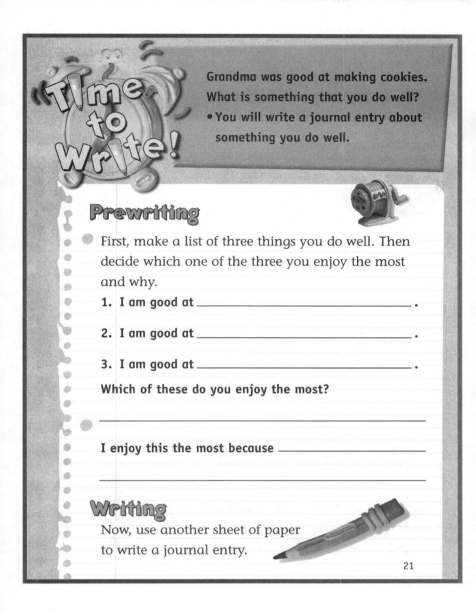

Time to Write!

Grandma was good at making cookies. What is something that you do well?

• You will write a journal entry about something you do well.

Prewriting

First, make a list of three things you do well. Then decide which one of the three you enjoy the most and why.

1. I am good at _____.

2. I am good at _____.

3. I am good at _____.

Which of these do you enjoy the most?

_____

I enjoy this the most because _____

_____

Writing

Now, use another sheet of paper to write a journal entry.

21

Prewriting

Explain to students that the prewriting activity will help them think about what they do well, and will help them get ready to write their journal entry.

Writing

Remind students to not only write about what they do well but also to explain why they enjoy doing this activity.

Sharing

Organize students into pairs. Have students in each pair share their journal entries with each other. Help students create journal covers for this and future writing activities out of poster board, string (to attach the cover to the inside paper and hold the spine together), markers, colored pencils, glitter, glue, and any other available materials.

Making Connections

Activity Links

• Have students demonstrate, describe, or draw pictures of something they do well for the class.

• Ask students to recall the room where the story takes place without looking at the illustrations in the selection. Have them rely on memory and imagination to draw pictures of the room, and ask them to label the items they show.

• Have students draw a picture of their favorite kind of cookie in the center of a sheet of paper. Around the picture, have students write as many words as they can think of that describe cookies.

Reading Links

You might want to include these books in a discussion about spending time with friends and families:

• *Aunt Flossie's Hats (And Crab Cakes Later)* by Elizabeth Fitzgerald Howard (Clarion Books, 1995).

• *Fireflies for Nathan* by Shulamith Levey Oppenheim (William Morrow, 1994).

• *We Are Friends* by Eve Feldman (Raintree Steck-Vaughn, 1998).

21

Strategy Focus

Visualizing to think about a selection.

Story at a Glance

A girl tries to find a quiet place to think.

Vocabulary

You may want to introduce the following words to your students:
garage
workbench
tickled
clover

Getting Students Started

- **Introducing the Selection**

Ask students where they like to go when they need to be alone to think. Have students talk about their "thinking places." Tell students that they are going to read a selection about a girl named Megan who needs to find a thinking place of her own.

- **Purpose for Reading**

Students read to find out what place Megan chooses to be her thinking place.

The Thinking Place

By Katie U. Vandergriff

Let's Read

This story is about a girl named Megan. She needs to find a quiet place to think. Read to find out where Megan can think.

"I think I need a place to think," said Megan to her sister, Kara.

"What do you need to think about?" asked Kara.

"Things," said Megan. "I like to think about lots of different things."

"Maybe you could go to your room. I go to my room when I want to think," Kara suggested.

22

"OK, I think I will try to think in my room," said Megan as she rushed off down the hall.

Megan shut her door and sat down on her bed.

 1 How do you think Megan's bedroom looks?

As soon as she started to think, she heard a loud noise. THUMP! THUMPA! THUMP! THUMPA! THUMP!

"Oh no!" said Megan. "Christopher is practicing on his drums!" She could not think at all with that noise.

23

Strategy Tip

Remind students that many stories we read include pictures to help us think about how people and events look. However, pictures cannot show us how everything we are reading about looks. Explain to students that it is important to make pictures in your head when there are no pictures on the page.

Possible Responses Question 1

Like a girl's bedroom.
Encourage this student to be more specific in his or her description. Ask, "What types of things are in a girl's bedroom?"

She has a bunk bed like mine.
This student is comparing his or her personal experience with Megan's to help visualize images from the reading. Ask, "What color is her bunk bed? What else are you picturing in the room?"

There is a bed.
This response lacks detail. To encourage this student to elaborate on his or her response, ask, "What does the bed look like? What else are you picturing in Megan's bedroom?"

Megan walked out to the garage. She sat down in her favorite old lawn chair. Just as she started to think, her dad walked in the door. "Hi, sweetie, what are you doing?" he asked.

"I am trying to think," said Megan.

"Well, the garage is a good place. I like to come here when I need to think, too," said her dad with a wink.

> **2** What are you thinking about now?

Possible Responses Question 2

The garage is a bad place to think.

This student has stated an opinion based on personal experience. Encourage the student to explain his or her response by asking, "Why do you think a garage would not be a good place to think?"

She should go to her tree house.

In this response, the student has stated an opinion. To find out if the student used personal experience to form this opinion, ask, "Is that where you go when you want to be alone to think? What might Megan's tree house look like?"

Where will Megan go to think?

Questioning the text reflects strong critical thinking skills. Encourage this student to answer his or her own question by making a prediction. Ask, "Where do you think Megan will find a quiet place to think?"

He walked over to the workbench, put on his safety glasses, and turned on the electric saw. WHEEEEEEENH! Z-Z-ZIP! went the saw as her dad pushed a board into the blade.

"Oh no!" said Megan. She could not think at all with that noise.

Megan walked into the kitchen. She sat down on the stool and sighed.

"What's the matter, darling?" asked her mother.

25

"I am trying to think," said Megan.

"The kitchen is a good place," said her mother. "I like to think in here." RATTLE, CLANK, RATTLE went the pots and pans. WHIRRRRRRRR went the mixer.

 3 What do you picture Megan's mother wearing?

26

Possible Responses Question 3

Probably a blue dress.
This response reflects the student's comprehension of the reading. Ask, "What else are you picturing Megan's mother wearing?"

She should wear an apron. Her clothes might get dirty.
In this response, the student is not only visualizing but is also using background knowledge to state an opinion about a scene from the story. Ask, "What are you picturing the apron looks like?"

Megan will go somewhere else.
Although this student has not answered the question, his or her response demonstrates good comprehension of the selection. He or she is making a prediction based on a pattern in the selection. Say, "You have made a good prediction. Can you also picture what Megan's mother is wearing?"

"Oh no!" said Megan. She could not think at all with that noise. She shook her head sadly and walked out into the backyard.

Megan sat down under the big tree and rested her head in her hands. "Where can I find a place to think?" she wondered. As she sat there, the grass tickled her feet, and she thought how good it felt. Megan lay down on her back in the shade and thought how the tree kept the sun from shining through. She watched the clouds blow by and wondered what made the clouds stay together.

27

Some cultures do not value or put an emphasis on the need for personal privacy. Some students may not have the background knowledge to understand the need for privacy and "alone time." Talk about the idea of needing time to oneself before students begin reading.

After Reading

It is very important to have students read and discuss what they pictured as they read, and what they wrote in response to the questions.

Discussing the Think-Alongs

- Give as many students as possible a chance to tell what they wrote in response to one of the questions.
- Have students explain what they were thinking when they wrote.
- Ask students how picturing what they read helps them think about the selection.

Reteaching

For those students who have not written or are having difficulty with the activity:

- Ask them to tell you what they were picturing as they read.
- Model your own use of visualization by sharing what you were thinking about as you read.
- Ask questions that motivate students to visualize, such as the following:
  - *What did you picture in Megan's garage?*
  - *What did you picture Megan's mom making in the kitchen?*
  - *How did you picture Megan's backyard?*
  - *How did you picture the tree?*

Megan smelled the fresh clover and flowers and thought about what made the flowers grow. She looked up at the big tree and said, "I think THIS will be my place to think!" Megan lay under the big tree and thought and thought and thought.

> **4**   What are you thinking about now?

28

Possible Responses Question 4

What is Megan thinking about?

Questioning the text reflects strong critical thinking skills. Encourage this student to use his or her own experiences to guess what Megan might be thinking about. Ask, "What kinds of things do you think about in your thinking place?"

Her brother might come out and bother her.

This student is drawing on information he or she learned from the story and is making a prediction based on the pattern established in the book. Ask, "What do you picture Megan saying to her brother if he bothers her?"

Megan needs to think.

This response summarizes a basic idea in the story. It is not clear from the response whether or not the student has a more in-depth understanding of the story. Say, "That's true. What is Megan trying to find throughout the story to help her think?"

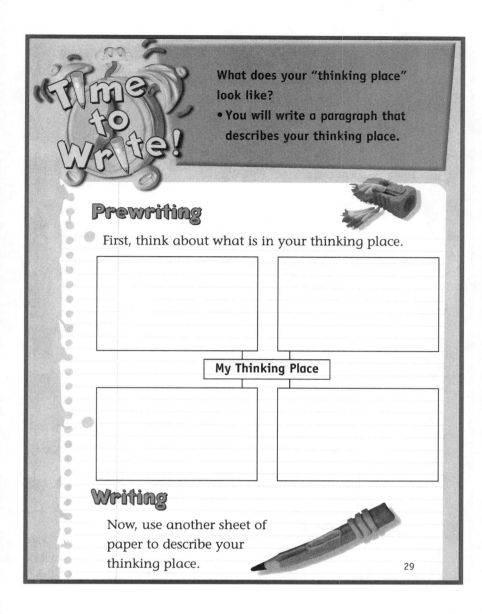

Time to Write!

What does your "thinking place" look like?
• You will write a paragraph that describes your thinking place.

Prewriting

First, think about what is in your thinking place.

My Thinking Place

Writing

Now, use another sheet of paper to describe your thinking place.

29

Prewriting

Explain that the prewriting activity will help students picture different objects in their own thinking places.

Writing

Remind students that their descriptions do not need to say where their thinking place is located. They should focus on describing their special thinking place.

Sharing

Have students read their descriptions to a partner. Have students guess where their partner's thinking place is based on his or her description.

Making Connections

Activity Links

• Have students draw pictures of different scenes in the selection.
• Designate a place in your classroom as a thinking place. Have students decorate it and make it a comfortable place to sit, think, and read.
• Have students create collages or posters that illustrate images of favorite thinking places, either real or imagined.

Reading Links

You might want to include these books in a discussion of how people think:
• *How Do We Think? (How Your Body Works)* by Carol Ballard (Raintree Steck-Vaughn, 1998).
• *Look Twice: Mirror Reflection, Logical Thinking* by Duncan Birmingham (Parkwest Publishers, 1993).
• *The Mind (Wonderful You)* by John Burstein (Fairview Press, 1996).

Thinking About...

Asking Questions

Generating Questions

Readers generate questions as they read. Generating questions helps readers think about what they already know and what they want to know about a selection. The activities in this unit will help students to think about and question what they are reading, thereby helping them to better understand and remember what they read.

Thinking About

Asking Questions

Read the story below. As you read, think about questions you might ask.

It was a cold morning. Kim's father turned on the oven. He got out a bowl. He put in muffin mix, an egg, and water. He stirred it all together. When the batter was smooth, he poured it into a muffin pan. The pan held eight muffins. He put the pan in the oven. Kim's family had hot muffins for breakfast.

30

Introducing the Strategy

Choose a story your students have read recently in class. Have students generate questions based on the story. You may need to give them some ideas at first. Expand the discussion to answer student questions and generate new ones. Explain that good readers think about questions that they have as they read.

Applying the Strategy

Ask students to follow along as you read the story in the pupil book, or have a volunteer read it. Tell them to think about what questions they would like to ask about the selection.

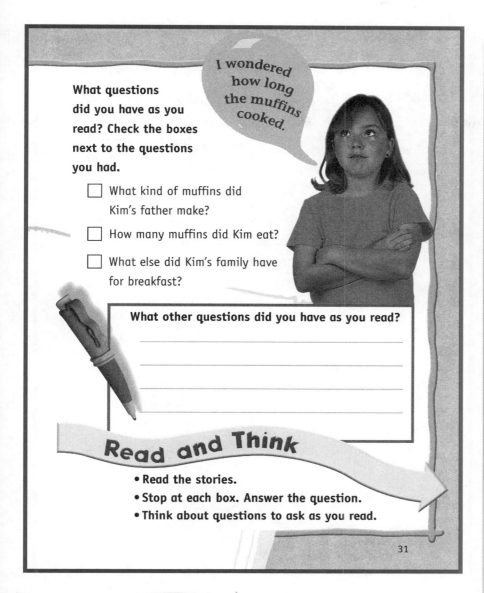

What questions did you have as you read? Check the boxes next to the questions you had.

I wondered how long the muffins cooked.

☐ What kind of muffins did Kim's father make?

☐ How many muffins did Kim eat?

☐ What else did Kim's family have for breakfast?

What other questions did you have as you read?

_____

_____

_____

_____

Read and Think

- Read the stories.
- Stop at each box. Answer the question.
- Think about questions to ask as you read.

31

Read and Think

- Remind students that answering the questions in the boxes will help them think about the selections.
- Tell them that they can write as little or as much as they need, or they can draw pictures to show what they are thinking.
- Encourage them to think about the questions they have as they read the selections.

Discussing the Strategy

Have students complete the questions independently or as a group. Ask students what they were thinking about while the story was read. Ask questions such as the following:

- *What might you ask Kim's father about cooking?*
- *What might you ask Kim about the muffins?*
- *What might you ask about what else they had for breakfast?*

Tell students that it is not important if they did not think of all the things in the list following the story. The important thing is that they thought about asking questions while they were reading.

Explain to students that they will use this strategy as they read the selections in this unit.

Strategy Focus

Generating questions to think about while reading a selection.

Story at a Glance

A boy learns to comfort himself and his baby brother.

Vocabulary

You may want to introduce the following words to your students:

music box	*rumbling*
lonely	*bubbling*
diapers	

Getting Students Started

• Introducing the Selection

Tell students that they are going to read a selection about a boy who knows what his new baby brother needs. Ask students to generate a list of things that babies need. Write this list on the board. Tell students that the selection will discuss many of the needs that they listed. It will also tell how Mama and Big Brother take care of the new baby.

• Purpose for Reading

Students read to find out what a little baby brother needs and how Big Brother helps take care of his baby brother.

A Big Brother Knows... What a Little Brother Needs

By Vashanti Rahaman

Let's Read

This story is about a boy and his new baby brother. Read to find out what a baby brother needs and how a big brother helps take care of him.

When my baby brother was born, everybody gave him presents—everybody except Daddy.

Daddy gave me a present. He gave me a little music box that played a soft, sleepytime song.

"It's for when you are lonely," he said. "Sometimes big brothers get a little lonely."

32

Strategy Tip
Tell students that thinking about what questions they might ask as they read will make reading the selection more interesting.

"How can I be lonely?" I thought. I was never lonely with just Mama and Daddy. And now there was Baby, too.

At first Baby slept a lot. Sometimes he cried, but Mama always knew why.

Sometimes Mama said, "He is hungry." And when she fed him, he stopped crying.

1 What question do you want to ask the boy?

33

Possible Responses
Question 1

Why do babies cry when they are hungry?
Students have many questions about babies, especially if they have had a new baby come into their families recently. This student's question shows that he or she is actively engaged with the reading and is curious about babies.

How did your mama know that he was hungry?
This student is asking an appropriate question about how babies communicate.

Ask, "What did the baby do to tell his mother that he needed something?"

Why do babies sleep so much?
This student is generating a question about babies based on a close reading of the text. Encourage students to discuss what babies need and how they communicate with their families.

"How did you know he was hungry?"
I asked Mama.

"I am his mama," she said. "I know."

Sometimes Mama said, "He needs to have his diapers changed." And when she changed him, he stopped crying.

2 What question do you want to ask Mama?

34

Possible Responses
Question 2

....

Does Daddy know a lot about babies, too?

This question would make a good topic for discussion. Say, "Some dads know a lot about babies. Do any dads you know help take care of babies?"

You know a lot about babies.

Although this response is not phrased as a question, it indicates that the student is comprehending the selection. Encourage the student to expand on this response by asking, "What makes you

think Mama knows a lot about babies? Is there a question you might ask Mama about taking care of babies?"

Can I help? That's what I ask my mom.

This student is generating a question based on personal experience. Ask, "How do you help your mom?"

"How did you know he needed changing?" I asked Mama.

"I am his mama," she said. "I know."

Sometimes she said, "His tummy hurts." And she lifted him up, patted his back, rubbed his tummy, and said, "There, there, Mama knows it hurts." Then, after a while, he made a little rumbling, bubbling noise and stopped crying.

3 What question do you want to ask Mama now?

35

Possible Responses
Question 3

Don't know.

Students may leave boxes blank, or may express confusion in their responses. Encourage students to write or draw a response in every box. Have this student re-read the previous section. Then ask, "Do you have any questions about babies?"

What does rumbling mean?

Students often respond to vocabulary and concepts they find difficult in a story. Encourage students to try to define words from context.

Walk around the room as students complete the activity so you can help them make sense of unfamiliar words. Say, "Rumbling means growling and rolling. Does your stomach ever rumble when you are hungry?"

What's wrong with the baby's tummy?

This question reflects comprehension of the story. Ask, "What do you think is wrong with the baby's tummy? How did the Mama help make the baby feel better?"

"It's a good thing he has a mama who knows," I said.

Sometimes Mama had to spend so much time with Baby that she couldn't play with me. Then, if Daddy was not home, I got a little lonely. But I had Daddy's music box. When I played it, I felt a little better. I was glad Daddy knew about big brothers getting lonely.

One day Baby kept crying and crying.

Mama fed him.

Mama changed him.

Mama patted his back, rubbed his tummy, and said, "There, there."

But, when she put him down on his play mat, he started crying again.

> **4** What question do you want to ask the baby?

36

Possible Responses
Question 4

. . . .

Why won't you stop crying? I don't like crying.
This student is not only generating a question based on a clear reading of the text, but he or she is also expressing an opinion and supporting it with personal experience.

cry fed cry changed cry patted cry
Students may respond to questions with single related words in a kind of free association. Encourage the student to clarify the ideas connecting these words by asking,

"What might you ask the baby about being fed and changed?"

What do you need now, baby?
This student mirrors key phrases in the text in generating this question. Ask, "What else do you think the baby might need?"

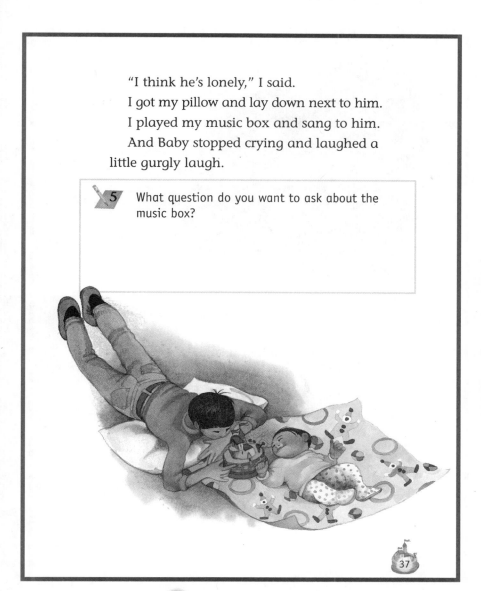

"I think he's lonely," I said.

I got my pillow and lay down next to him.

I played my music box and sang to him.

And Baby stopped crying and laughed a little gurgly laugh.

> **5** What question do you want to ask about the music box?

37

Ask students to write down on large self-stick notes three things that babies need. Have students re-read the selection and place their notes on the pages that mention those needs. Ask students to record what Mama and Big Brother do in the story to meet those needs.

Possible Responses
Question 5

Why doesn't the baby have his own music box?

This question shows that the student is understanding the selection, is paying attention to details, and is applying critical thinking skills. Ask, "Do you think the big brother likes to share his music box with the baby?"

What song was in the music box?

This question reflects a close reading of the story and an attention to details. Ask, "Do you know any songs that might be good sleepy time songs for a music box?"

Why is the baby lonely?

Although this student has not addressed the question, he or she is generating a thoughtful question about a point made in this section of the reading. Ask, "Do you ever get lonely when your mother wants you to play by yourself?"

After Reading

It is very important to have students read and discuss the questions they have written in the boxes.

Discussing the Think-Alongs

- Give as many students as possible a chance to tell what they wrote in one of the boxes.
- Have students explain what they were thinking when they wrote.
- Ask students how asking questions helps them better understand the selection.

Reteaching

For those students who have not written or are having difficulty with the activity:

- Ask them to tell what they were thinking about as they read.
- Model this stragegy for students by generating questions about the selection as you read, and sharing these questions with students.
- Ask questions that encourage students to generate their own questions about the selection, such as the following:
  - *What might the baby brother ask his mama if he could talk?*
  - *What might the baby brother ask his big brother if he could talk?*
  - *What questions might you ask Mama about taking care of a baby?*
  - *What questions might you ask Big Brother about taking care of a baby brother?*

"How did you know that he was lonely?" asked Mama.

"I am his big brother," I said. "I know."

Mama hugged me and gave me a big kiss. "It is a good thing that he has a big brother who knows," she said.

38

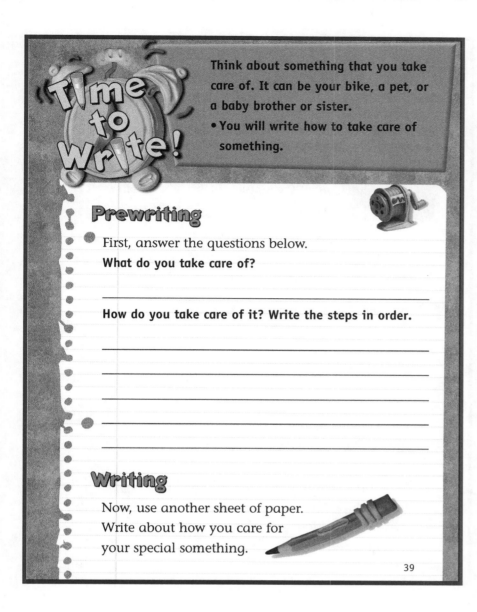

Time to Write!

Think about something that you take care of. It can be your bike, a pet, or a baby brother or sister.

• You will write how to take care of something.

Prewriting

First, answer the questions below.

What do you take care of?

_____

How do you take care of it? Write the steps in order.

_____

_____

_____

_____

_____

Writing

Now, use another sheet of paper. Write about how you care for your special something.

39

Prewriting

Explain that the prewriting activity will help students organize their thoughts about taking care of a special object, animal, or person. Tell them that this will make it easier for them to write about taking care of their special something.

Writing

Remind students that they should describe how they take care of their special something as clearly as possible so that someone else could easily take good care of their special something if they go away on vacation.

Sharing

Organize students into pairs and have them read their descriptions to each other. Encourage students to give feedback to their partners, pointing out clear and unclear parts of their descriptions.

Making Connections

Activity Links

• Ask students to illustrate their descriptions of how to take care of their special something.

• Plan a field trip to a local daycare center or invite a parent with an infant to visit the class. Have students generate questions they would like to ask about babies and how to take care of them.

• Give students scenarios of things that could happen while taking care of a baby. Have students role play what they would do in each situation, using a doll.

Reading Links

You might want to include these books in a discussion about caring for babies:

• *The New Baby* by Mercer Mayer (Golden Books, 1983).

• *Carl's Afternoon in the Park* by Alexander Day (Green Tiger Press, 1995).

• *Love You Forever* by Robert Munsch (Firefly Press, 1985).

Strategy Focus

Generating questions to think about while reading a selection.

Story at a Glance

This selection describes the making of the Statue of Liberty.

Vocabulary

You may want to introduce the following words to your students:

statue   *freedom*
skyscraper   *torch*
liberty   *pedestal*

Getting Students Started

- **Introducing the Selection**

Tell students that they are going to read a selection about the making of the Statue of Liberty. Ask students to tell what they know about the Statue of Liberty. (For example: It is big, in New York, has a torch, and so forth.) Write these facts on the chalkboard. Then ask students to generate a list of questions about the Statue of Liberty. Tell students that the selection will answer some questions about the statue, such as how it was made and who made it.

- **Purpose for Reading**

Students read to find out what the Statue of Liberty is and how it was made.

The Statue of Liberty

By Lucille Recht Penner

This story tells how the Statue of Liberty was made. Read to find out what the Statue of Liberty is and how it was made.

A lady stands in the New York Harbor. She is as tall as a skyscraper. She is called the Statue of Liberty.

> **1**   What question do you want to ask about the Statue of Liberty?

"Liberty" means freedom. All over the world, people dreamed of coming to America to find freedom.

People came by ship. The trip took many days. Men, women, and children were crowded together. They were tired, hungry, and scared.

40

Possible Responses
Question 1

What is a harbor?

Students often respond to vocabulary and concepts they find difficult in a selection. Encourage them to try to define words from context. Walk around the room as students complete the activity so you can help them make sense of unfamiliar words.

I wonder how the statue stands up so tall.

While this student has not generated a response in question form, the response still reflects a questioning of the selection. Encourage the student to look for the answer to this question as he or she continues reading.

Why is it called the Statue of Liberty?

This student is generating a typical question. Say, "That's a good question. See if you can find the answer to your question as you read."

Strategy Tip

Tell students that thinking about questions they might ask as they read will make reading "The Statue of Liberty" more fun.

Suddenly they saw the lady! They had reached America at last. Now they knew they were free. People cried for joy.

The Statue of Liberty was a present from the people of France to the people of the United States.

A Frenchman made the lady. His name was Frédéric Bartholdi. He copied his mother's face for his statue. How beautiful she was!

2 What question do you want to ask Frédéric Bartholdi?

41

Possible Responses
Question 2

Why did you make the statue?
In asking this question, the student is looking for an explanation of a cause-and-effect relationship. Encourage the student to look for the answer to this question as he or she reads the text, or help the student find the answer in a trip to the school library.

Why did you copy your mother's face? I would too, because my mom is pretty.
In this response, the student asks a question, expresses an opinion, and compares his or her personal experience with Bartholdi's.

Oh, liberty means free. I bet the people were glad to be free.
While this student does not offer a question response, he or she has found the answer to a question about the meaning of a word. Encourage students to answer their questions and generate new ones as they read. Say, "Yes, liberty does mean freedom. What questions might the people coming to America have?"

Pair students acquiring English with fluent English speakers. Ask students to make a list of difficult words from the selection, starting with the vocabulary list. Have students write the vocabulary words in both the non-native English speaker's language and in English. Ask students to discuss the meanings of these words, drawing pictures to represent difficult words such as *harbor, skyscraper,* and *crates.*

First Frédéric made a small statue.

Then a bigger one.

Then an even bigger one.

The last statue was so big it could not fit in his workshop!

He had to make it in pieces. He made the right hand holding the torch. Then he made the head.

Each finger was longer than a man. Each eye was as big as a child.

Frédéric needed lots of help. His helpers worked in a big room.

They took the pieces outside and put them together. She was higher than all the buildings. Much higher!

42

Workers took the statue apart. They packed it in 214 crates.

A ship carried it from France to New York. In America the people were building a high pedestal for the lady to stand on.

But they ran out of money! The work stopped. No one knew what to do.

Joseph Pulitzer owned a newspaper. He had an idea.

3 What question do you want to ask about making the statue?

43

Possible Responses
Question 3

Why did he make bigger and bigger statues?

This question reflects a close reading of the text. Say, "That's a very interesting question. Do you think it would be hard to make a really big statue without practicing?" Discuss with students why Bartholdi might have made models of the statue.

What is his idea?

This question reflects good reading comprehension.

Did they use glue to put the statue together?

This question reflects the use of personal experience to relate to the reading, and shows a close reading of the text. Encourage this student to read more about how the Statue of Liberty was put together during a class trip to the school library.

Remind students that they can use the strategies they have already learned, such as visualizing. For example, discuss with students what they think the Statue of Liberty looked like on the day when Frédéric Bartholdi presented her to the world. Encourage students to describe how they picture the statue's face, her torch, the stairs that Bartholdi climbed, and the cheering crowds of onlookers.

Joseph said, "The statue needs a home! I will print the name of everyone who gives money to help."

Thousands of people sent nickels and dimes. Children sent pennies. Soon there was enough money.

Now workers could finish the huge pedestal. They set the lady on top of it.

4 What are you thinking about now?

44

Possible Responses Question 4

Did Joseph print all the names?

This student is learning to independently generate questions. Encourage the student to write a likely answer to his or her question beside his or her original response.

Why did they need a pedestal?

In this response, the student is generating a question that asks for an explanation of a cause-and-effect relationship.

send money build statue

Students may respond to questions with a string of single words in a kind of free association. To encourage the student to combine these words into a more coherent statement or question, ask, "Can you tell me more about what you were thinking when you wrote these words?"

A big French flag was draped over her face.

On October 28, 1886, the people of New York had a parade to welcome her.

The President of the United States made a speech. Frédéric Bartholdi was excited! He raced up a staircase inside the statue. Up and up he went to the very top.

> **5** What question do you want to ask Frédéric Bartholdi?

45

Possible Responses
Question 5

Did you feel tired running up all those stairs?

This student has asked a question that reflects good reading comprehension. Ask, "Would you be tired after running up all those stairs?"

What did the president give a speech about?

This question reflects strong critical thinking skills. Encourage the student to write some ideas about what the president might have talked about in his speech beside his or her original response.

Why was a French flag over her face?

This student's question reflects good reading comprehension. Encourage the student to write a possible answer to his or her question beside his or her original response.

After Reading

It is very important to have students read and discuss the questions they have written in the boxes.

Discussing the Think-Alongs

- Give as many students as possible a chance to tell what they wrote in one of the boxes.
- Have students explain what they were thinking when they wrote.
- Ask students how asking questions helps them better understand the selection.

Reteaching

For those students who have not written or are having difficulty with the activity:

- Ask them to tell what they were thinking about as they read.
- Model the questioning strategy by asking questions as you read the selection and sharing them with students.
- Ask students questions that encourage them to generate their own questions about the selection, such as the following:
  - *What might you ask Frédéric Bartholdi about making the Statue of Liberty?*
  - *What might you ask Joseph Pulitzer about helping to finish the Statue of Liberty?*
  - *What might you ask Frédéric Bartholdi about the day he pulled the flag off the Statue of Liberty?*
  - *What might you ask the people who first saw the Statue of Liberty in New York Harbor?*

Frédéric looked down. A boy was waving a white handkerchief. It was the signal. Frédéric pulled a rope and the flag fell.

There was the lady! Hip, hip, hurrah! Cannons boomed. Boat whistles blew. People cheered.

The excitement never ended. Today, more than one hundred years later, the Statue of Liberty still welcomes people to America— the land of the free.

> **6** What are you thinking about now?

46

Possible Responses Question 6

Don't know.
This student did not produce a meaningful response to the question. Encourage a response in every box. Ask, "Why do you think the people were so excited about the Statue of Liberty? Would you be excited to see it?"

How does it welcome?
This question reflects good reading comprehension. Say, "That is a good question. Why do you think the statue is a welcoming sight for people coming to America?"

I want to see the Statue of Liberty.
This student is responding personally to the story, which reflects an active engagement with the reading.

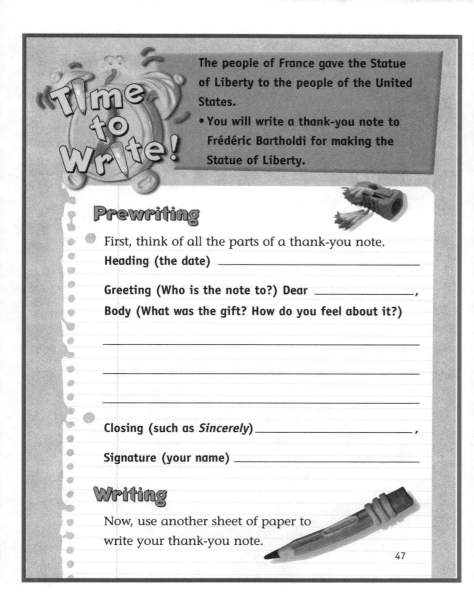

Time to Write!

The people of France gave the Statue of Liberty to the people of the United States.

• You will write a thank-you note to Frédéric Bartholdi for making the Statue of Liberty.

Prewriting

First, think of all the parts of a thank-you note.

Heading (the date) _____

Greeting (Who is the note to?) Dear _____ ,

Body (What was the gift? How do you feel about it?)

_____

_____

_____

Closing (such as *Sincerely*) _____ ,

Signature (your name) _____

Writing

Now, use another sheet of paper to write your thank-you note.

47

Prewriting

Explain that the prewriting activity will help students think about all parts of a thank-you note. This will help them organize their thoughts and write a better note.

Writing

Remind students to include all parts of the thank-you note (heading, greeting, body, closing, and signature). Tell them that their notes need to be as clear as possible so that the people receiving the notes understand what the students are trying to say.

Sharing

When students have finished writing their thank-you notes, organize them into pairs. Have the members of each pair take turns reading each other's notes. Ask students to tell their partners which sections of the notes are confusing or need clarification, and have them help their partners improve their notes.

Making Connections

Activity Links

• Ask students to illustrate their thank-you notes. Encourage them to draw pictures of the Statue of Liberty and people welcoming her to New York and the United States.

• Plan a field trip to a local art museum. Before leaving, have students look through picture books about famous artists and the artwork they will see at the museum, including sculptors. Discuss the works they saw at the museum.

• Have students create their own sculptures from clay. After they have created their own sculptures, discuss with students what they think it would have been like to sculpt the Statue of Liberty. Ask the school's art teacher to assist in this activity.

Reading Links

You might want to include these books in a discussion of famous artists and inventors:

• *Alexander Calder* by Mike Venezia (Children's Press, 1998).

• *The Art Lesson* by Tomie DePaola (Paper Star, 1997).

• *Camille and the Sunflowers: A Story About Vincent Van Gogh* by Laurence Anholt (Barrons Juveniles, 1994).

Strategy Focus

Generating questions to think about while reading a selection.

Story at a Glance

A young detective solves the case of his brother's missing lunch.

Vocabulary

You may want to introduce the following words to your students:
problem
sandwich
pickle (as in "in a pickle")
jam (as in "in a jam")

Getting Students Started

• Introducing the Selection

Tell students that they are going to read a selection about a boy named Sam. Sam solves the case of the missing lunch for his brother, Rick. Ask students to think about a time they could not find something. Ask students questions such as the following:
– *What was missing?*
– *Did you ever find it?*
– *Where was it and how did it get there?*

• Purpose for Reading

Students read to find out how Sam solves the case of the missing lunch.

The Case of the Missing Lunch

By Jean Groce

This story is about a young detective named Sam. Read the story to find out how Sam solves the case of the missing lunch.

It was a slow day at the office. There wasn't enough work to do. I needed a case. Something to make me think. Something to make me feel like singing.

Shortly after noon, I heard someone at the door.

It was a boy I knew. He looked sad.

48

"I need your help," he said.

"You've come to the right place!" I sang.

"Got a problem?

Lost your cat?

Sam can find it

just like that!"

 1 What question do you want to ask Sam?

"Tell me about it," I said, taking out my pen. "First of all, what's your name?"

"You know my name," the boy said. "I'm your brother."

49

Strategy Tip

Tell students that thinking about what questions they might ask Sam and Rick as they read will make reading the story more fun.

Possible Responses
Question 1

How do you find things?
The student has generated a question based on the reading. Encourage students to answer these questions for themselves as they read. Say, "Look for the answer to your question about how Sam finds things as you read on."

I wonder why Sam is singing.
While this student has not generated a response in question form, the response still reflects a questioning of the selection. Ask, "Why do you think Sam is singing?"

How do you know?
Perhaps this student is questioning whether Sam really can "find it just like that." However, this is not clear from what the student has written. Ask the student to elaborate by asking, "How does Sam know what?"

This selection contains some idiomatic expressions that may seem strange to students whose first language is not English, or to native English speakers who have not heard them before. Phrases such as "in a pickle" and "in a jam" can be amusing. Make a list of other American idiomatic expressions (such as "couch potato" and "Don't count your chickens before they hatch.") and have students think of similar expressions from their own languages to share with the class.

"All the same, you have to tell me your name," I said. "That's how it's done."

"All right," he said. "My name is Rick."

I wrote the name on my pad. "Now, Rick, tell me your problem," I said.

"My problem is my lunch," Rick said. "It's gone!"

 2   What question do you want to ask Rick?

50

Possible Responses
Question 2

Did you eat it?
This response is appropriate, yet brief. Say, "That is a good question. Do you think Rick ate the lunch? If he did, why did he come to Sam for help?"

Rick's lunch is gone. Why?
This student has restated the general idea of this section of the reading by stating the problem and asking why the problem exists. Ask, "Where do you think Rick's lunch might be?"

Did somebody take it? Dad took mine by accident once.
Students often use more than one strategy at a time. This student is not only generating a question but is also connecting the situation in the reading to personal experience. Ask, "Who do you think might have taken Rick's sandwich?"

I wrote *lunch* and *gone* on my pad. "That's not odd," I said. "Lunches are always gone after you eat them."

"I didn't eat it!" Rick said. "I made a big, beautiful sandwich. I went to get a glass of milk. When I came back to the table, the sandwich was gone! Can you help me find my lunch?"

"Sure!" I sang.

> *"In a pickle? In a jam?*
> *The one you need to call is Sam!"*

Rick put his hands over his ears. "That is enough singing!" he said. "Your songs are too silly!"

51

"Sorry," I said. "I always sing. I can't help it. Anyway, let's go."

 3 What are you thinking about now?

"Where are we going?" Rick asked.

"To see your plate," I told him. "Show me where you eat lunch."

Rick started to laugh. "You know where I eat lunch," he said. "You live in the same house!"

"All the same, you have to take me there. That's how it's done."

Rick and I went home. There was the plate on the table. I gave it a long look. I didn't see a sandwich.

52

Possible Responses
Question 3

Why do you like singing?
This response indicates that this student is learning to independently generate questions without being prompted to do so. Ask, "Do you like to sing? Why do you think that Sam might like to sing?"

lunch gone Sam help
Students may respond to questions with single related words in a free association. This kind of response is appropriate, particularly since this reflects the notes Sam makes on his pad in the story. This type of response not only helps students get their ideas down quickly but also helps them develop their understanding of the sequence of events.

Sam's going to look for clues.
This student is making a prediction about what might happen next. Ask, "What makes you think he is going to look for clues?"

"I hope you find my sandwich soon,"
Rick said. "I'm hungry!"

I needed an idea, and I needed it fast.

I looked around. Soon I had seen what
I was looking for.

 4 What question do you want to ask Sam?

I ran next door to borrow three things.
Then I ran back home.

"I think I know where your sandwich is,"
I called to Rick. "Watch!"

I put some dog food in a dish in front of
Happy. He gave it one sniff and went back
to sleep.

53

Meeting Individual Needs

Ask students to make a list of clues that led Sam to realize that the dog must have eaten Rick's sandwich. Have students think about what Sam did and saw that proved to him that the dog ate the sandwich.

Possible Responses
Question 4

What were you looking for?
This is a typical question response. At this point in the selection it is not clear what Sam has seen. Ask the student to try to answer his or her own question by asking, "What do you think Sam was looking for?"

Don't know.
This student has not produced a meaningful response to the question. Students may also leave boxes blank. Encourage students to write a response in every box. Ask this student, "What do you think Sam saw in the kitchen?"

I think he saw who stole the sandwich.
Although this student has not generated a question, this response shows that the student is comprehending the selection and making predictions about what might have happened. Ask, "What would you like to ask Sam about who stole the sandwich?"

After Reading

It is very important to have students read and discuss the questions they have written in the boxes.

Discussing the Think-Alongs

- Give as many students as possible a chance to tell what they wrote in one of the boxes.
- Have students explain what they were thinking when they wrote.
- Ask students how asking questions helps them better understand the selection.
- Encourage students to try to answer their own or other students' questions.

Reteaching

For those students who have not written or are having difficulty with the activity:

- Ask them to tell what they were thinking about as they read.
- Model how you generate questions by asking questions as you read the selection aloud and share the questions with students.
- Ask questions that encourage students to generate their own questions about the selection, such as the following:
  - *What would you ask Sam about being a detective?*
  - *What would you ask Sam about how he solved the case?*
  - *What would you ask Rick about what happened to his sandwich?*

"I knew it! He isn't hungry because he's already eaten," I said. "I'm sorry about your sandwich, Rick, but Happy ate it! See the peanut butter on him?"

I made Rick a new sandwich. Then I wrote *Case Closed* on my pad while I sang,
*"Now you're no longer in a jam.
Aren't you glad you called on Sam?"*

 5 What are you thinking about now?

54

Possible Responses Question 5

My dog does that. He eats stuff he's not supposed to. Then he looks guilty.
This student is visualizing how the dog in the story must look by relating the story to personal experience. Ask, "How do you think Sam figured out that Happy ate the sandwich?"

What is Sam going to do next?
This student is learning to generate questions independently. Encourage the student to answer his or her own question by asking, "What do you think Sam might do next?"

I like peanut butter, too.
This response indicates that the student is focusing on a detail in the selection and is making a personal connection to the reading. Encourage the student to also think about the main idea of the selection by asking, "How did Sam solve the case of the missing peanut butter sandwich?"

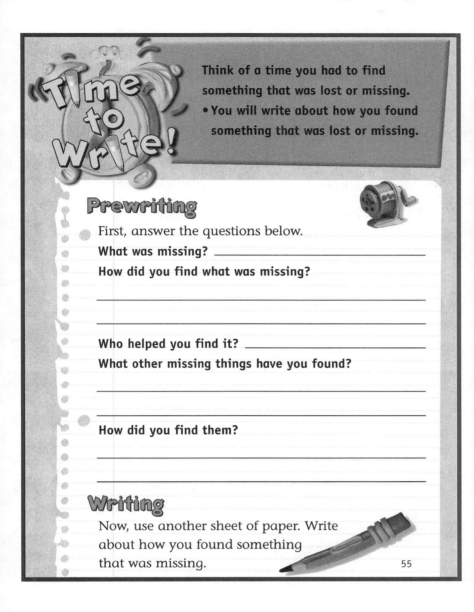

"Time to Write!"

Think of a time you had to find something that was lost or missing.
• You will write about how you found something that was lost or missing.

Prewriting

First, answer the questions below.

What was missing? _____

How did you find what was missing?

_____

_____

Who helped you find it? _____

What other missing things have you found?

_____

_____

How did you find them?

_____

_____

Writing

Now, use another sheet of paper. Write about how you found something that was missing.

55

Making Connections

Activity Links

• Have students play a guessing game similar to twenty questions. Assign one student to be "It" and to think of a person, object, or place with which the other students are familiar. Have students ask questions that can be answered "yes" or "no." When the class has guessed what the person, place, or object is, have another student be "It."

• Show students pictures from *The Mysteries of Harris Burdick* by Chris Van Allsburg and Harris Burdick. Have students create their own stories to explain what is happening in the pictures.

• Read aloud a mystery or detective story, stopping at various points to ask students what they think will happen next.

Reading Links

You might want to include these books in a discussion of other mystery and detective stories:

• *The Mysteries of Harris Burdick* by Chris Van Allsburg and Harris Burdick (Houghton Mifflin, 1984).
• *The ABC Mystery* by Doug Cushman (HarperCollins Publishers, 1996).
• *The Case of the Crooked Candles* by Jonathan Cann (Raintree/Steck-Vaughn, 1998).

Prewriting

Explain to students that the prewriting activity will help them organize their thoughts about a time when they discovered something was missing, and how they found the object. Tell them that this will help them write about the missing object.

Writing

Remind students that they should write about a time when they found something that was missing. Tell students that they can write about finding something that belonged to them, or a time when they helped find something that belonged to a friend, parent, or relative.

Sharing

When students have finished the writing activity, have them share what they have written with the rest of the class. Then have students draw pictures showing what they did to find what was missing.

The Tests

The next three selections are like standardized-test reading comprehension passages, with questions at the end of each selection. However, boxes with think-along questions appear within the selections to allow students to practice their think-along strategies.

Note that these selections are not designed to test specific reading strategies, but rather are designed to show students how thinking along will help them comprehend what they are reading and better answer questions about what they have read.

Introducing the Tests to Students

Ask students to share their ideas about test taking, such as how they go about answering multiple-choice questions. They may say that they read the selection and then answer the questions at the end. Tell them that for these selections, they will apply the think-along process, stopping at certain places in the text to answer questions. Point out that thinking about what they are reading as they read will make answering questions at the end of the story easier. Have students begin reading the selections on their own, answering the questions in the boxes and at the end of the selection.

Thinking Along on Tests

- Read each story.
- Stop at each box. Answer the question.
- Answer the questions at the end of each story.

What does Grace get for her birthday?

"Happy birthday, Grace!" her brother Adam yelled. "Dad is bringing your present home with him! It's a pet! And it begins with the same letter as your name, *g*."

"Oh!" Grace cried. "What is it?"

 1   What are you thinking about now?

HAPPY BIRTHDAY

56

Possible Responses
Question 1

I think it's a garter snake.
This student uses Adam's clue to guess what pet Grace might get for her birthday. Say, "That's a good guess. What other animals' names start with *g*?"

I got a dog for my birthday once.
This student is connecting personal experience to the reading. Ask, "Do you think Grace is going to get a dog? What clue does Adam give that helps you think about

what kind of pet Grace might get?"

I don't like people who tell secrets!
This student states an opinion about the events in the story by connecting them with personal experience. Ask, "Why don't you like people who tell secrets? Do you think Grace will guess what her father is bringing her for her birthday and ruin the surprise?"

"It's not a gorilla!" Adam said.

"Is it a goose?" Grace asked.

"No. It's not a goat, either." Adam winked at Mom.

When Dad got home, he had a big glass bowl. He filled the bowl with water.

Then Dad took out a bag of water with a goldfish in it. He put it into the bowl. The fish swam around and around.

"Oh, goodie!" Grace cried.

"That's a great name," Adam said. "We can call it Goodie."

"No," Grace said. "I will call it Goldie, not Goodie."

"Great!" Adam said, smiling. "Another name that begins with g."

 2 What are you thinking about now?

57

The Selections and Questions

The three selections in this test section are of different types: two fictional stories and one expository article. Each is followed by four multiple-choice questions and one short-answer question. The question format is typical of many standardized and criterion-referenced tests. The purpose-setting question format at the beginning of each selection is similar to that used on many nationally standardized tests. These questions help students to focus on a purpose for reading.

Possible Responses
Question 2

A gorilla would be neater!
This student is comparing an animal mentioned earlier in the reading with the pet that Grace has received, which reflects strong reading skills. Ask, "Can you think of other pets that begin with *g* that weren't talked about in the story?"

Too many g's!
This student is expressing a personal reaction to the alliteration used by the author. Ask, "Why do you think there are too many *g's* in this story?"

Encourage students to read the story aloud to see how they handle the alliteration.

Goldfish are pretty when they swim around in glass bowls or tanks.
This student is visualizing how the goldfish in the story might look by connecting the story to personal experience. Ask, "Have you seen other kinds of fish, too?"

Darken the circle for the correct answer.

1. Dad is bringing home a

    _____.

  Ⓐ bicycle

  Ⓑ name

  Ⓒ pet

  Ⓓ picture

3. What letter is most important in this story?

  Ⓐ *h*

  Ⓑ *b*

  Ⓒ *s*

  Ⓓ *g*

2. Who is having a birthday?

  Ⓐ Adam

  Ⓑ Grace

  Ⓒ Dad

  Ⓓ Mom

4. Dad's gift was a _____.

  Ⓐ gorilla

  Ⓑ giraffe

  Ⓒ goat

  Ⓓ goldfish

Write your answer on the lines below.

5. How does Adam feel at the beginning of the story?

_____

_____

_____

Answers and Analysis

1. C; literal
2. B; literal
3. D; evaluative/critical
4. D; literal
5. Evaluative/critical.

Responses could include one or more of the following:

- Adam is just trying to have fun.
- Adam is excited about Grace's birthday present.
- Adam is jealous and he wants the present.
- Adam loves knowing something Grace doesn't know.
- Adam is teasing his sister by winking at Mom.

Scoring Question 5:

2 = An answer that assigns one of these possible assumptions about Adam's behavior.

0 = An answer that tells what Adam did, but does not tell how he might have felt.

Explanation of Comprehension Skills

Literal: The answer is specifically stated in the text.
Inferential: The answer can be inferred from the text, but it is not specifically stated.
Evaluative/Critical: The answer is based on an evaluation of the text.

What is a polliwog?

There is a very old story about a frog. In the story, the frog turns into a prince. But do you know what turns into a frog? It is a tadpole.

A tadpole comes from an egg that a frog lays in the water. A tadpole has a tiny round body with a long tail. It has no legs at first. A tadpole lives under water. It breathes like a fish.

 1 What are you thinking about now?

Another name for a tadpole is *polliwog.* The last part of that funny name came from the word *wiggle.* That is how a polliwog, or tadpole, swims. It wiggles its way through the water.

59

Possible Responses
Question 1

I've seen those! They are neat!
This student has connected personal experience to the reading, and has expressed a personal reaction to the subject matter. Ask, "What did you think was neat about them?"

I like that story! The prince is cool.
This student is connecting a detail in the reading with personal experience reading another story. Ask, "Why do you think the prince is cool?" Ask students familiar with the story alluded to in this selection to tell the story to classmates who are unfamiliar with the story.

I didn't know frogs lay eggs!
This is an enthusiastic response in which the student expresses a personal reaction to information learned from the reading. Ask, "What other animals lay eggs?"

A tadpole and a caterpillar both change into something else. A caterpillar changes into a butterfly. A tadpole changes into a frog.

A tadpole first begins to grow little legs. As its legs grow, its tail gets smaller. It soon has lungs that it will use when it hops out of water as a frog. Finally, a tadpole loses its tail. Then it looks just like a tiny frog.

It is fun to watch a tadpole become a frog. You can't watch a frog become a prince. That is just a story you can read. It never really happens. But you can watch tadpoles turn into frogs!

 2 What are you thinking about now?

Possible Responses
Question 2

I can see them wiggling.
This student is visualizing the information provided in the text. Ask, "What do the tadpoles look like? How are they shaped?"

I want to read more about butterflies.
This student is asking for information beyond what the story provides. Encourage him or her to read more about butterflies during a visit to the school library.

Flying frogs! I can see that!
This student is creatively visualizing frogs doing many things. Ask, "What do the frogs you are imagining look like as they fly? Do any frogs really fly? How do most frogs move around?"

Darken the circle for the correct answer.

6. Part of the word *polliwog* comes from the word _____.

   Ⓐ *swim*
   Ⓑ *change*
   Ⓒ *tail*
   Ⓓ *wiggle*

7. A caterpillar and a tadpole both _____.

   Ⓐ become butterflies
   Ⓑ turn into princes
   Ⓒ change into something else
   Ⓓ swim under water

8. A polliwog becomes a _____.

   Ⓐ butterfly
   Ⓑ frog
   Ⓒ caterpillar
   Ⓓ prince

9. A frog needs lungs because it _____.

   Ⓐ must swim under water
   Ⓑ uses them to wiggle
   Ⓒ needs them to fly
   Ⓓ will hop onto land

Write your answer on the lines below.

10. How does a tadpole change?

_____

_____

_____

_____

61

Answers and Analysis

6. D; literal
7. C; literal
8. B; inferential
9. D; literal
10. Evaluative/critical. Responses could include one or more of the following:
   - It begins to grow legs.
   - It gets lungs.
   - Its tail gets smaller.
   - It turns into a little frog.

Scoring Question 10:

2 = Answers that include one or more of the possible responses listed above.

0 = Answers that don't provide either the main idea (tadpoles turn into frogs) or two accurate details.

Explanation of Comprehension Skills

Literal: The answer is specifically stated in the text.
Inferential: The answer can be inferred from the text, but it is not specifically stated.
Evaluative/Critical: The answer is based on an evaluation of the text.

What did Sara and Yolanda get at the yard sale?

The people in the neighborhood were planning a yard sale. They wanted to raise money for the new library. Mrs. McCann was in charge. Sara and Yolanda were helping.

Sara and Yolanda wanted to bring some things to sell. But they couldn't think of anything they wanted to give up.

1 What are you thinking about now?

Sara and Yolanda talked about what they could bring to the sale. "I was thinking about giving my baseball glove," Yolanda told Sara. "I haven't used it for a while. But it's the one I used when we won the big game. I just don't think I can give it away."

62

Possible Responses
Question 1

It would be hard to give stuff up!

This response shows the student empathizing with the characters by expressing a personal reaction to the story. Ask, "Have you ever had a yard sale? Have you ever been to one?"

Is the library in trouble?

This student may not understand the idea of giving to a charitable cause. Explain that when a new library opens, it often needs more money than it has in order to offer people more books and other services. People help raise money to make the library a better place.

I don't think they want to sell their stuff. I wouldn't.

This student is making a prediction based on a personal reaction to the story. Ask, "How do you think the girls would feel if they gave something to the yard sale?"

Sara said she had a game she might bring. "Mom thinks I should give it to the sale. I really like that old game," she told Yolanda. "I played it with my mom and dad and sister and brother. It's too important to give away."

 2 What are you thinking about now?

The two girls left each other and went home to look for something for the yard sale. A little while later, Yolanda and Sara were back at Mrs. McCann's house. Yolanda was carrying a baseball glove. Sara had a game under her arm.

"These are the things we want to give to the yard sale," the girls told Mrs. McCann. "We want to help get money for the library."

63

Possible Responses
Question 2

I don't think they should give those away! Can't they find toys they don't want?
This response shows comprehension of the main idea of this part of the story. The idea of sacrificing for the interests of people who need help can be pursued in discussion. Ask, "Why do you think they might want to give some of their things to the garage sale?"

They can make money. I sold a game at my neighbor's sale.
This student is connecting personal experience to the reading. Ask, "Do you think the girls should sell their baseball glove and game at the yard sale to make money for the library?"

They are going to be sorry!
This student makes a prediction about how the girls will react after they sell their things at the yard sale. Ask, "What makes you think they will be sorry?"

On the day of the sale, Yolanda's baseball glove sold quickly. She did not see who bought it. Then the girls noticed that Sara's game was gone. Someone had bought it.

After the sale, the girls found out that Sara's dad had bought Yolanda's baseball glove to give to Sara. And Yolanda's mom had bought Sara's game to give to Yolanda.

Yolanda said, "I got your game."

Sara said, "I got your baseball glove."

They both asked at the same time, "Want to trade?"

 3   What are you thinking about now?

Possible Responses
Question 3

What was she doing all day? She should know who got it.
This is a critical response that generates a question about the events described in the story. Encourage the student to try to answer his or her own question by asking, "What do you think she was doing all day?"

Did their parents know they would trade?
This student has generated a question based on an analysis of story events. Ask, "Do you think their parents will mind if they trade?"

The library got money and they got to keep their stuff!
This summary response indicates a thoughtful reading of the story and an understanding of the main idea.

Darken the circle for the correct answer.

11. What were the people in the neighborhood planning?
   Ⓐ a baseball game
   Ⓑ a yard sale
   Ⓒ a trip to the library
   Ⓓ a picnic

12. How did Yolanda feel about her baseball glove?
   Ⓐ She wanted to sell it.
   Ⓑ She didn't really want to sell it.
   Ⓒ She wanted Sara to have it.
   Ⓓ She was very tired of it.

13. What did Sara sell at the yard sale?
   Ⓐ a game
   Ⓑ a box
   Ⓒ a baseball glove
   Ⓓ a garage

14. Who bought the baseball glove?
   Ⓐ Yolanda's mom
   Ⓑ Sara's dad
   Ⓒ Mrs. McCann
   Ⓓ Yolanda

Write your answer on the lines below.

15. Do you think Sara and Yolanda were happy or sad at the end of the story? Why?

_____

_____

_____

65

Making Connections

Discussion

After the students have completed the questions for all three selections, discuss with them what they wrote in the boxes. Ask students to tell what they wrote in a box and to explain why they wrote what they did. Then, have students discuss how writing in the boxes helped them to remember what the selection was about so they could better answer the questions at the end of the selections.

For your own curricular planning, you might also want to review what students have written in the boxes. Reading what students have written will give you an idea of how well they are comprehending what they read and whether they need additional review of the process of thinking along as they read.

Scoring

Refer to the discussion of test taking on page T11 of the teacher's edition for information on scoring and interpreting student scores.

Answers and Analysis

11. B; literal
12. B; literal
13. A; literal
14. B; literal
15. Evaluative/critical.
Answers may include one or more of the following points:
- The girls are probably very happy because they are getting back the things they reluctantly donated to the yard sale.
- The girls can feel good about having given favorite items to help with the sale.

Scoring Question 15:
2 = An answer that notes that the girls are happy that each will probably get her donation back.
0 = An answer that attributes feelings to the girls that the story does not suggest.

Explanation of Comprehension Skills
Literal: The answer is specifically stated in the text.
Inferential: The answer can be inferred from the text, but it is not specifically stated.
Evaluative/Critical: The answer is based on an evaluation of the text.

Thinking About...

Details and Main Ideas

Understanding Details and Main Ideas

Every selection has one or more main ideas. Each main idea is supported by details that provide additional information about the main idea. The activities in this unit will help students apply the strategy of understanding details and main ideas, thereby helping them understand and remember what they read.

Details and Main Ideas

Read the story below. As you read, think about the details and main idea of the story.

Dan has a big red box. He keeps special things inside it. He likes to take his special things out and look at them. He finds the blue ribbon he won for his model car. He looks at the picture of his friend John. Dan sees tiny white sneakers. He wore them when he was a baby. Dan puts everything back in the box. Then he puts the box back in the closet.

special things

66

Introducing the Strategy

Choose a selection your students have read recently in class. Use a selection that is rich with details. Remind the students what the selection is about and ask them to recall some details that were in the selection. Talk about how the details add descriptive information about an object, tell more about a character, or describe specific events that happened during the story. Explain that good readers think about details and main ideas when they read.

Applying the Strategy

Ask students to follow along as you read the story in the pupil book, or have a volunteer read it. Tell them to think about the details and main idea as you read.

Check the boxes next to the special things that were in Dan's box.

This story made me think of my special things.

☐ red sneakers

☐ blue ribbon

☐ mittens

☐ picture of a boy

What is the story mainly about?

_____

_____

_____

Read and Think

- **Read the stories.**
- **Stop at each box. Answer the question.**
- **Think about details and main ideas.**

67

Discussing the Strategy

Have students complete the questions independently or as a group. Ask students what they were thinking while the story was read. Ask questions such as the following:

- *What was Dan thinking about when he looked at the objects in his big red box?*
- *Do you have a special place where you put your favorite things?*

Tell students that it is not important if they did not think of all the things in the list following the story. The important thing is that they thought about the details and main idea while they were reading.

Explain to students that they will use this strategy as they read the selections in this unit.

Read and Think

- Remind students that answering the questions in the boxes will help them think about the selections.
- Tell them that they may be using other strategies as they read, such as making predictions, connecting personal experiences, or generating questions.
- Encourage them to think about details and main ideas as they read the selections.

Strategy Focus

Understanding main ideas and details.

Story at a Glance

A girl who is too little to walk her big dog finds a way to take him for a walk.

Vocabulary

You may want to introduce the following words to your students:

scratched   cocker spaniel
poodle   drooped
beagle   apartment

Getting Students Started

• Introducing the Selection

Ask students if they have ever been told by their parents or others that they are too little to do something. Then ask if they ever tried to find a way to show their parents that they really could do it. Tell students that in this selection a girl figures out how to do something that her parents did not think she could do.

• Purpose for Reading

Students read to discover how Jessie solves the problem of being too little to take her dog, Bart, for a walk.

Jessie's Big Idea

By Carolyn Short

 This story is about Jessie. She wants to walk her dog, Bart. Read the story to learn about Jessie's plan to walk Bart.

Jessie loved Bart. She played catch with him. She fed him. She filled his bowl with water. She brushed his shiny coat. She scratched him behind the ears.

> **1** How did Jessie show that she loved Bart?

68

 Possible Responses
Question 1

She took care of him.
This student has summarized the main idea. To encourage the student to discuss some details from the story, ask, "What were some of the things Jessie did to take care of Bart?"

This reminds me of my dog that I have to take care of just like Jessie does.
This student has compared his or her personal experience with Jessie's. Encourage the student to address the question more directly by asking, "What are some of the things that you and Jessie have to do to take care of your dogs?"

She feeds him, plays with him, gives him water, but she doesn't take him for a walk.
In this response, the student shows comprehension of the story's details. Ask, "Why do you think she doesn't take him for a walk?"

Jessie did almost everything for Bart. But there was one thing Jessie couldn't do. She couldn't walk Bart.

"You're too little to walk that big dog," said Dad.

"You can walk him when you're bigger," said Mom.

So every day, Dad walked Bart. Jessie walked with them. When she saw her friend Allison walking her little white poodle, she would smile and say, "Hi, Allison! Hi, Gigi!"

When she saw her friend Conner walking his beagle, she would wave and shout, "Hello, Conner! Hello, Floppy!"

69

Strategy Tip

Tell students that every story has a main idea, as well as details that help clarify the main idea. Tell them that it is important that they look for the main ideas and the details in a story as they read.

When she saw her friend Mandy walking
her cocker spaniel, she would call out
"Hello, Mandy! Hello, Ginger!"

If only Bart were as little as her friends'
dogs, she would be able to walk him.

 2 Why could Jessie's friends walk their dogs?

Possible Responses
Question 2

*Maybe their moms let them
and Jessie's mom won't let
her.*

Although this is a thoughtful
response in which the student is comparing and contrasting, he or she has missed
the detail about the size of
the dogs. Ask, "What is different about the other dogs?"

*Bart would pull Jessie
around.*

While this student is not
addressing the question, he
or she is stating one of the
main ideas based on an

understanding about why
Jessie is not allowed to walk
Bart. Ask, "What is different
about Jessie's friends' dogs
and Bart?"

*The other dogs were smaller
than Bart?*

This student has stated the
main idea in question form.
Say, "Yes, that is true. What
did you read that tells you
that the other dogs are
smaller than Bart?"

One day Dad was too sick to walk Bart. "I'll walk him," said Mom. But just as they were leaving, the phone rang. Grandma needed Mom right away.

"I'm sorry, Bart," said Mom. "I guess you won't get a walk today." Bart's tail drooped. Bart's ears drooped. Even Bart's eyes drooped. He stood by the door and whined.

71

ESOL

Have students acquiring English tell the names of different animals in their first language. In addition, ask them to share some of the common names that are given to various pets in their culture. Have them draw pictures of several pets. Then ask them to label their pictures with pet names in their first language and in English.

"Poor Bart," said Jessie. "You want to go for a walk, don't you?" She rolled a ball to Bart, but Bart didn't want to play. He lay down on his blanket.

"Poor Bart," said Jessie. "I wish I could walk you." Jessie brushed Bart's back. She brushed Bart's side. She even brushed Bart's tail, but the big dog just stared sadly at the door.

 3 Why was Bart so sad?

72

Possible Responses
Question 3

He couldn't go for a walk.

Bart wanted to go out and nobody took him.

Each of these responses indicates an understanding of the main idea. Ask, "What did Bart do to show he wanted to go for a walk?"

Because he was sad.

In this response, it is unclear whether the student understands the main idea because he or she has only repeated the idea in the question. To encourage a more thoughtful response, ask, "Why do you think Bart was sad? What did Bart want?"

"Poor Bart," said Jessie. "If I were bigger..." Jessie stopped. She had an idea. She called Allison and Conner and Mandy on the telephone.

The three friends arrived at Jessie's apartment. Each of them carried a leash. Jessie found Bart's leash. She fastened the four leashes to Bart's collar. Bart's eyes sparkled. Bart's ears perked up. Bart's tail wagged.

4   What do you think Jessie is planning to do?

73

Reinforcing the Strategies

Ask students to visualize how Jessie and her friends take Bart for a walk. Ask students to describe how the four leashes attach to Bart's collar and how the children look as they walk Bart. Then have them draw this scene.

Possible Responses
Question 4
....

They are going to walk Bart.
This student has made an accurate prediction. Ask, "What happened in the story that makes you think they are all going to take Bart for a walk?"

Jessie's friends came to her apartment.
In this response the student has summarized what has just happened in the story, but has not predicted what the characters are planning to do next. Ask, "Why do you think all of Jessie's friends came to her apartment? What did they bring with them?"

Bart is happy.
This student has summarized one main idea from this section, but has not predicted what Jessie plans to do. Ask, "Why do you think Bart is happy? What do you think Jessie and her friends are going to do?"

After Reading

It is very important to have students read and discuss the main ideas and details they thought about as they read the selection.

Discussing the Think-Alongs

- Ask students to review the details that helped them to understand the following main points:
  - *Jessie loved Bart.*
  - *Bart was sad he couldn't go for a walk.*
  - *Jessie tried to make Bart happy when he couldn't go for a walk.*
- Ask students to tell what Jessie's problem is in the story. Tell them that a problem is often the main idea in a story.
- Ask students how Jessie solved the problem in the story. Tell them that the main idea in many stories involves someone solving a problem.

Reteaching

For those students who have not written or are having difficulty with the activity:

- Ask them to draw pictures that illustrate the main events in the story.
- Have students underline the details that show that Bart was sad because he was not going for a walk.
- Read one of the sections aloud and ask students to tell as many things as they can about Bart. Ask questions such as the following:
  - *How does Bart feel?*
  - *What does Bart look like?*
  - *What is happening to Bart?*

"What's going on?" asked Mom, walking into the apartment.

"Mom, may we walk Bart?" asked Jessie.

Mom looked at the big happy dog and the four happy friends. "What a clever idea," she said. "May I follow along?"

"Yes!" shouted Jessie.

"Woof!" barked Bart.

> **5** How did everyone feel when they went for a walk?

74

Possible Responses
Question 5

I wonder if Bart will pull all of the kids around?
Although this student has not directly addressed the question, he or she has anticipated what might happen next. Ask, "Why do you think Mom asked if she could go along? How do you think the kids felt when they took Bart for a walk?"

They are going to have a lot of fun. Bart is very happy.
This response offers a prediction based on a main idea from this section of the reading.

Ask, "Why do you think they are going to have lots of fun? Why is Bart going to be so happy?"

They were all happy.
Like the previous response, this student has stated the main idea of this section of the reading. Ask, "What problem did Jessie have at the beginning of the story and how did she solve the problem at the end?"

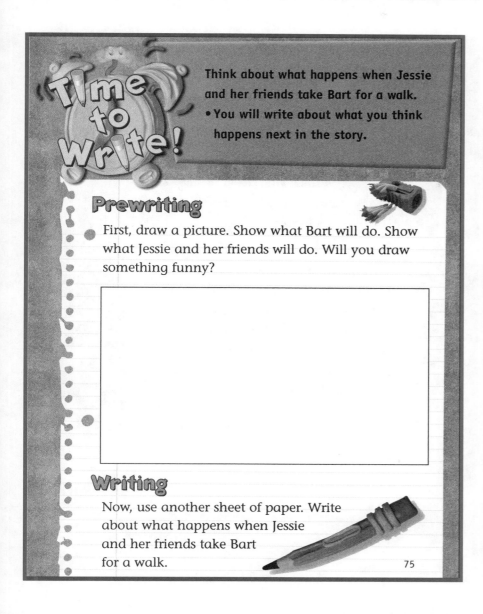

Time to Write!

Think about what happens when Jessie and her friends take Bart for a walk.
- You will write about what you think happens next in the story.

Prewriting

First, draw a picture. Show what Bart will do. Show what Jessie and her friends will do. Will you draw something funny?

Writing

Now, use another sheet of paper. Write about what happens when Jessie and her friends take Bart for a walk.

75

Making Connections

Activity Links

- Have students tell the class about the ways they take care of pets at home. Ask them to draw pictures showing how they care for their animals.
- Ask students to write about all of the places in their neighborhood where they might take a dog for a walk. Encourage students to use details when telling about these places.
- Have students collect pictures of dogs from magazines and newspapers to display on a bulletin board. Help them find out which dogs are large and which are small. Group the pictures on the bulletin board by the size of the dogs: big, medium, and small.

Reading Links

You may want to include these books in a discussion about children and their dogs:
- ***Aaron's Awful Allergies*** by Troon Harrison (Kids Can Press, 1998).
- ***Arthur's New Puppy*** by Marc Tolon Brown (Little Brown, 1998).
- ***Fletcher and the Great Big Dog*** by Jane Kopper Hilleary and Richard Eric Brown (Contributor) (Sandpiper, 1992).

Prewriting

Explain to students that drawing a picture will help them think about what they will write. Encourage them to think about what they are going to write as they draw their pictures. Tell them that drawing is a good way to think of ideas for writing.

Writing

Remind students that they need to think about what has happened so far in the story and what they are going to tell about what might happen next. Ask them to think about the following questions:

- *Will your story be funny?*
- *How will Bart feel?*
- *What will Jessie and her friends do?*

Sharing

Ask students to read their stories to the class or to each other in small groups. Have students compile their stories in a class book. A title for the collection of stories might be "Jessie and Bart's Walk."

Strategy Focus

Understanding main ideas and details.

Story at a Glance

This selection tells about what various animals do during the winter to stay warm and to find enough to eat.

Vocabulary

You may want to introduce the following words to your students:
woodchuck
fox
geese
Canada

Getting Students Started

- **Introducing the Selection**

Ask students if they know how animals get ready for the winter. Discuss why animals have to get ready for winter. Emphasize the cold and the lack of food. Tell them that this selection tells about how different animals get ready for the winter.

- **Purpose for Reading**

Students read to learn how different animals get ready for the winter.

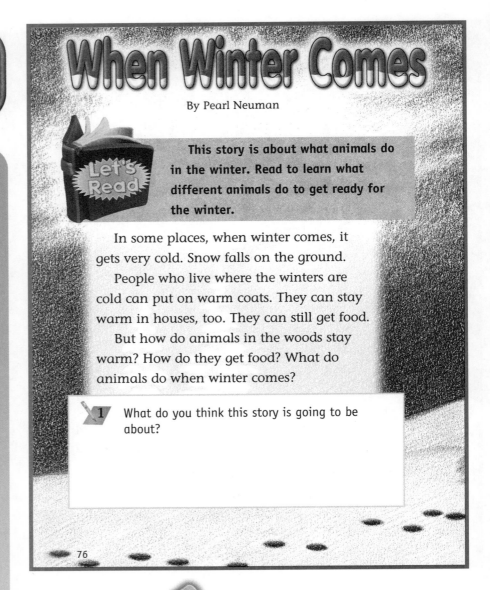

When Winter Comes

By Pearl Neuman

Let's Read

This story is about what animals do in the winter. Read to learn what different animals do to get ready for the winter.

In some places, when winter comes, it gets very cold. Snow falls on the ground.

People who live where the winters are cold can put on warm coats. They can stay warm in houses, too. They can still get food.

But how do animals in the woods stay warm? How do they get food? What do animals do when winter comes?

1 What do you think this story is going to be about?

76

Possible Responses
Question 1

It's going to tell about winter. This student has a general idea of the main concept. Encourage the student to be more specific about the main idea by asking, "What do you think the story is going to tell us about winter?"

How people live in the winter. In this response, the student has restated one of the main points made in an opening paragraph of the reading, but has inaccurately predicted the story's main focus. Ask,

"What else do you think this story will tell about?"

What animals do in the winter. This response indicates a good understanding of the main idea. Ask, "What are some of the things the animals have to take care of in winter?"

Here is a woodchuck with grass in its mouth. It uses the grass to make a nest under the ground.

When it has made the nest, the woodchuck eats lots of the grass and green leaves. By the time winter comes, the woodchuck is fat.

On the very first cold day, the woodchuck goes into its nest. It takes some grass and uses it to plug up the hole to the outside.

77

Strategy Tip

Tell students that this article will tell how different animals get ready for the winter. Tell them that some parts of stories describe details and other parts describe main ideas. Tell them that it is important to tell the difference between main ideas and details when they read.

Then the woodchuck closes its eyes, curls up in a ball, and goes to sleep.

The woodchuck sleeps all winter long. It sleeps all day and all night. It doesn't need to go out or get up to eat. It lives on its fat all winter long.

2 How does the woodchuck get ready for winter?

78

Possible Responses
Question 2

It makes a nest and sleeps all winter.

They get fat and go to sleep for the winter.

Both of these responses indicate an understanding of the main idea of the section. Ask these students, "What do you think it would be like to sleep all winter?"

I wonder how they can sleep all winter?

In this response, the student shows an understanding of the main idea and questions information not provided in the text. Help this student find more information about animal hibernation during a trip to the school library.

Here is a black bear out for a walk. Before the first snow, it must find somewhere to sleep. The black bear looks for a safe place in a cave or a log. It looks for a good spot under the trees.

The black bear finds a place to sleep. Now it is set for the winter. It has a home where it can spend the cold days. The black bear sleeps on a grass bed. It sleeps in the day, and it sleeps at night, too.

79

Meeting Individual Needs

Have students draw pictures of all the animals that save food during the summer so that they have food to eat in the winter, or ask them to draw pictures of animals that sleep during the winter. Have them write captions for their pictures. Sleeping animals include opossums, fish, turtles, snakes, lizards, and some mammals. Animals that save food or eat extra food to get ready for winter include squirrels, chipmunks, raccoons, and other small mammals. Many larger mammals also eat extra food to fatten up for the winter.

But the black bear does not sleep as long as the woodchuck does. The woodchuck sleeps all winter. The black bear wakes up from time to time. On some days, the black bear leaves its cave and goes looking for plants or animals to eat.

3 What does the black bear do for most of the winter?

Possible Responses
Question 3

I thought bears slept all winter.
Although this student has not directly answered the question, he or she understands the main idea and is comparing and contrasting this idea with background knowledge. Ask, "What do bears do in the winter besides sleep?"

I would hate to meet a black bear in the woods.
While this student has expressed an opinion in reaction to the reading, he or she has not addressed the question. Encourage the student to think about the main idea by asking, "Do you think you would meet a black bear in the woods in the winter? What do black bears do during most of the winter?"

We saw bears at the zoo.
This student is relating personal experience to the reading but has not addressed the question. Ask, "What do bears who live in the forest do in the winter?"

Here is a red fox at work before winter. It digs a deep hole to hide some of its food. It packs away food for the winter, when it is hard to find food.

On a very cold winter night, the red fox will come back to where it hid the food. The fox will dig up the food that it had packed away.

On winter days that are warm, the red fox will go out to look for fresh food. On a walk in the woods, the fox sees a mouse. The red fox dives down in the snow to try and grab the mouse. The mouse can be food for the red fox.

 4 What does the red fox do to get ready for winter?

81

Have students acquiring English share with the class what animals in their country of origin do in the winter. Encourage them to teach the class how to say the names of these animals in the student's first language.

Possible Responses
Question 4

- -

He catches mice.

In this response, the student has understood and stated one detail from the section, but it is not clear that he or she has grasped the main idea. Ask, "Why does the fox catch mice? What is the fox doing to be sure he can live through the winter?"

He hides food for the winter.

The fox hides food and finds food so he will have something to eat all winter.

These students have summarized the main idea in this section and one student has added some detail. If students have difficulty summarizing the main idea in this section, ask, "What is the fox doing to get ready for winter?"

Here are some birds that fly south for the winter. The birds are called Canada geese. When winter comes, they fly south from Canada to Florida or California.

Why do Canada geese fly south? In winter, it is hard for the geese to find food. It is cold and the plants they like to eat stop growing. It is warm in the south. There are plants there for the geese to eat. They fly south to find food.

82

We know this because people in Canada sometimes put out food for the geese. When they do, the geese stay in Canada for the winter.

In the summer, the geese fly back to the north. In the summer it is hard for the geese to find food and water in the south. It is very dry there. The geese fly north to Canada to find food.

> **5** Why do the geese fly south in winter?

Possible Responses
Question 5

· ·

All of the birds fly south in the winter.

This student has understood one aspect of the main idea. Encourage the student to re-read these two pages, and ask, "Why do some geese stay in Canada during the winter? What are the geese looking for when they fly south?"

Where is Canada?

Although this student has not addressed the question, he or she understands that knowing Canada's location is important. Show students Canada's location on a map and discuss Canada's winter weather. Then ask, "What does the story say about why geese fly south for the winter?"

They like to go where it is warm and where there is food to eat.

This response reflects thorough comprehension of the main idea and details presented in this section of the reading.

It is very important to have students read and discuss the main ideas and details they thought about as they read the selection.

Discussing the Think-Alongs

- Ask students to tell the main idea about what each animal in the selection does in winter, and describe the details about how each animal gets ready for winter.
- Have students explain what they were thinking when they wrote.
- Ask students how looking for the main idea and details in the story helped them better understand the selection.

Reteaching

For those students who have not written or are having difficulty with the activity:

- Ask each student to draw a picture of one of the four animals discussed in the story in winter.
- Model the strategy by pointing out the main idea and important details as you read the selection aloud.
- Ask questions such as the following:
  - *Why does a woodchuck eat so much grass before winter?*
  - *How does the black bear get ready for winter?*
  - *What does the red fox do during the winter?*
  - *What do geese do to get ready for winter?*

What do animals do in the winter? Some sleep like the woodchuck. Some sleep and wake like the bear. Some pack away food like the red fox does. When there's no food, some leave home like the Canada geese.

Each animal does what it needs to do to stay warm and get food when winter comes.

6 What do the animals do in the winter?

84

Possible Responses
Question 6

They do lots of things to keep warm and eat enough.
The student has briefly summarized the main idea. Encourage the student to discuss some of the details by asking, "Can you tell about some of the things that animals do to keep warm and have enough to eat during the winter?"

I wouldn't like to be an animal in the winter.
This student has empathized with animals' struggles to stay alive during the winter.

Encourage the student to summarize the main idea of this section by asking, "What are some of the things you could do if you were an animal facing a cold, snowy winter?"

There were lots of animals in the story.
This student may be confused about the main ideas in this story. Ask, "What are some of the things that the story said animals do during the winter? What do they eat? How do they stay warm?"

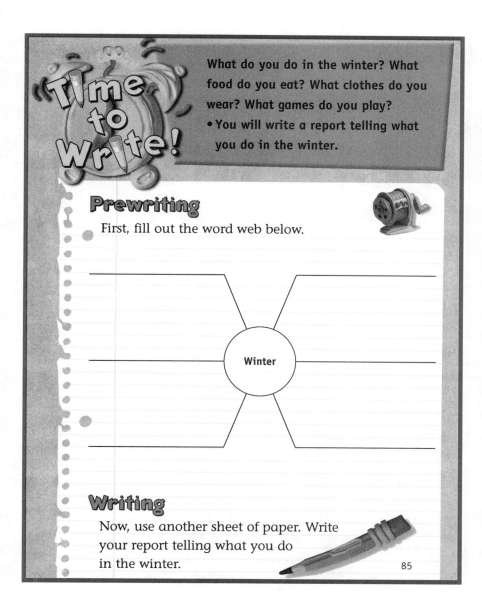

Time to Write!

What do you do in the winter? What food do you eat? What clothes do you wear? What games do you play?
• You will write a report telling what you do in the winter.

Prewriting

First, fill out the word web below.

Winter

Writing

Now, use another sheet of paper. Write your report telling what you do in the winter.

85

Making Connections

Activity Links

• Have each student pick a particular animal to study. Ask them to find out all they can about what that animal does in the winter. Have them make a collage featuring their animal and using pictures that they find in magazines or books.

• Ask student volunteers to pantomime different animals preparing for winter. Have other students guess which animals their classmates are pantomiming.

• Have students keep a list of all the animals they see on their way to and from school. Discuss what these animals do to get ready for winter. Even cats and dogs grow thicker coats for winter, and some get fatter.

Reading Links

You may want to include these books in a discussion about animals in winter:

• *What Do Animals Do in Winter?: How Animals Survive the Cold* (*Discovery Readers*) by Melvin Berger, Gilda Berger (Contributor) (Ideal Children's Books, 1995).

• *Animals in the Snow* by Margaret Wise Brown (Hyperion Press, 1995).

• *Fang, the Story of a Fox in Winter* (*Animals Through the Year*) by Kenneth Lilly (Raintree/ Steck-Vaughn, 1997).

Prewriting

Explain to students that the prewriting activity will help them think about what they and their families do during the winter. For those unfamiliar with cold and snow, you might discuss what they think they would do if they lived where it was cold and snowy in the winter.

Writing

Remind students that their report should be interesting and clearly explained so that someone who reads it knows about all of the things they might do in the winter.

Sharing

Organize students into small groups. Have students take turns reading their reports out loud to each other. Encourage students to help each other identify parts of their reports that need clarification. You may want to gather the final reports into a class book titled *Things We Do in the Winter*.

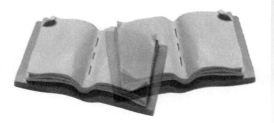

A Gift to Share

A Gift to Share

Strategy Focus

Understanding main ideas and details.

Story at a Glance

A girl who does not have enough money to buy a present for her aunt makes a book of photos to share.

Vocabulary

You may want to introduce the following words to your students:

piggy bank   mail carrier
magazine   photos
vase

Getting Students Started

• **Introducing the Selection**

Tell students they are going to read a story about a girl named Mattie who doesn't have enough money to buy a birthday gift for her Aunt Debra. Ask students what they would do if they were Mattie. Tell them that in this selection Mattie finds a way to give her Aunt "the best gift ever."

• **Purpose for Reading**

Students read to find out what Mattie does so she can give Aunt Debra a birthday gift.

A Gift to Share
By Barbara Swett Burt

Let's Read

This story is about a girl named Mattie. She wants to give the best gift ever to her Aunt Debra. Read to find out what she gives Aunt Debra.

Soon it would be Aunt Debra's birthday. Everyone in Mattie's family had a present for her, except Mattie. She thought all week about what to give Aunt Debra. She wanted to give her the best gift ever.

86

Mattie knew Aunt Debra would love a new book. Mattie shook her piggy bank. She had only $1.78. That would not be enough to buy a new book. Mattie thought hard. What could she get Aunt Debra?

 1 What do you think Mattie is going to do?

Mattie saw her brother and asked, "What do you think would be the best gift ever?"

He said, "A football, of course."

Mattie said, "Thanks, but I don't think that's the best gift ever." She knew Aunt Debra wouldn't want a football. Mattie thought hard. What could she get her?

87

Strategy Tip

Tell students that every story has a main idea as well as details that help clarify the main idea. Tell them that it is important that they look for the main ideas and the details in a story as they read.

Possible Responses
Question 1

Ask mom for more money.
This student has made a prediction based on the personal experience that parents are a source for money. To encourage the student to focus on the main idea, ask, "What do you think she could get for Aunt Debra?"

Get a cheaper book.
This prediction reflects a close reading of the story. Ask, "Why do think she's going to get a cheaper book?"

Buy a card and candy.
This response indicates that the student has read and understood the details. Ask, "Is $1.78 enough money to buy both a card and candy?"

Have the students cut out pictures from magazines or catalogs that show all kinds of gifts. Then have them group the gifts in one or more categories, such as the following: gifts for adults or children, large or small gifts, or gifts that can be worn or played with. Alternatively, have students organize the gifts by the first letter of the name of the gift. Have students make posters on which they display the different groups of gifts.

Next, Mattie saw her cousin. Mattie asked, "What do you think would be the best gift ever?"

He said, "A car, of course."

Mattie said, "Thanks, but that's not the best gift ever." She knew she couldn't buy Aunt Debra a car. Mattie thought hard. What could she get her?

Mattie ran to the store and found Aunt Debra's favorite magazine. Mattie hoped she would have enough money. But it cost too much. Mattie thought hard. What could she get Aunt Debra?

88

Mattie asked Mom, "What do you think would be the best gift ever?"

Mom said, "Well, sometimes the best gifts are the ones that come from the heart. Could you make something yourself?"

> **2** What kind of gift could Mattie make?

Mattie thought hard. What could she make? She could make a vase, but she didn't have any clay. She could paint a picture, but she didn't have any paint. She went outside to take a walk and think some more.

89

Possible Responses
Question 2

Maybe her mom will help her.
Although this prediction may be based on personal experience, this student has not directly addressed the question. The student needs to recognize that Mattie is trying to figure out what kind of present to give her aunt. Ask, "What did her brother, cousin, and mother suggest as a gift for Aunt Debra?"

a napkin holder
This response shows that the student understands the main idea and is using personal experience to relate to the story. Ask, "What else can Mattie make for her aunt?"

a picture or a necklace
In this response, the student uses personal experience to predict a few things that Mattie might make her aunt.

She walked toward Aunt Debra's house. She saw the mail carrier handing two boxes to her aunt. Aunt Debra said, "Great! They're here. I've been waiting for my new books. I just love to read."

Mattie watched Aunt Debra open the boxes. Her aunt held the books with special care. Mattie smiled. This gave her a great idea. She thought, "I can make a book about me for Aunt Debra to read." She turned and ran home. She just knew that would be the best gift ever.

 3 What are you thinking about now?

Possible Responses
Question 3

She will make a book.
In this response the student summarizes the main idea of this section. Ask, "What do you think Mattie is going to put in the book?"

Mattie will write a story about herself for the book.
This response provides details to support the main idea in the selection. Ask, "What kind of story will she write?"

I don't know.
Encourage students to write a response in every box. To prompt this student to restate the main idea, ask, "What is Mattie going to make for her aunt?"

Mattie ran upstairs to her room. She got out her favorite book to see how it was made. Then she got out her art supplies and a box of photos. Mattie picked out her brightest crayons and her best paper. She also picked out some special photos.

91

Have students tell about special gift-giving traditions in their culture. Ask them to draw pictures of these gift-giving occasions, and have them write captions for their pictures in their first language and in English.

Mattie folded the papers. She wrote a title on the first page. She glued photos on the next pages. She printed words in her best writing. She glued her favorite photo to the front for the cover. Then she wrapped the book in pretty paper.

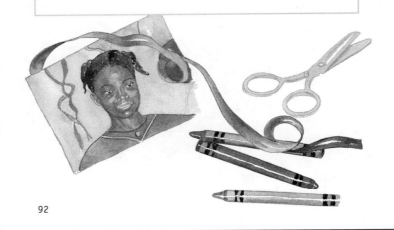

4 What do you think will happen when Aunt Debra sees Mattie's book?

Possible Responses
Question 4

She will be happy.

She's going to tell Mattie that the book is nice.

She will smile.

All three responses are predictions that show the students understand how Aunt Debra will react. Ask, "Why do you think Aunt Debra will be happy? What do you think Mattie will say to Aunt Debra? What do you think Aunt Debra will say to Mattie?"

The next day, Mattie gave Aunt Debra her gift. When Aunt Debra opened it, a huge smile filled her face. She said, "This book is so special! It's better than any book I could ever buy." They looked at each photo of Mattie.

93

This selection is useful for asking students to visualize the contents of the book that Mattie made. Ask students to describe the kinds of pictures Mattie included in her book and what kinds of words she wrote in the book.

It is very important to have students read and discuss the main ideas and details they thought about as they read the selection.

Discussing the Think-Alongs

- Give as many students as possible a chance to tell what they wrote in one of the boxes.
- Have students explain what they were thinking when they wrote.
- Ask students what problem Mattie faced in the story. Tell them that a problem is often the main idea in a story. Ask them how understanding the main idea helps them better understand the selection.

Reteaching

For those students who have not written or are having difficulty with the activity:

- Ask them to tell what they were thinking about as they read.
- Have them underline the details that show some of the ideas that Mattie had about a gift for Aunt Debra.
- Ask questions that help students identify the main idea in the story, such as the following:
    - *What did Mattie want to do for Aunt Debra's birthday?*
    - *What did Mattie's mother suggest that she do?*
    - *What kind of gift did Mattie give to Aunt Debra?*
    - *How did Aunt Debra feel about the gift?*

Then Mattie had an idea. She found a photo of herself and Aunt Debra sitting together. She glued it on the last page. Aunt Debra looked at the photo and said, "Now the book is about us, too. This is the best gift ever."

 5 Why is the book "the best gift ever"?

94

Possible Responses Question 5

nice pictures
The student has stated one of the details that make the book a nice gift, but the response is somewhat vague. Encourage this student to focus on the main idea by asking, "Who is in the pictures? Why are these pictures so important to Aunt Debra?"

They are both in it.
In this response, the student has summarized the main idea of this section of the story. Ask, "Why do you think that Aunt Debra likes the book with pictures of herself and Mattie in it?"

Because she made it herself.
This student has stated the main idea. Ask, "How did Mattie make the book special?"

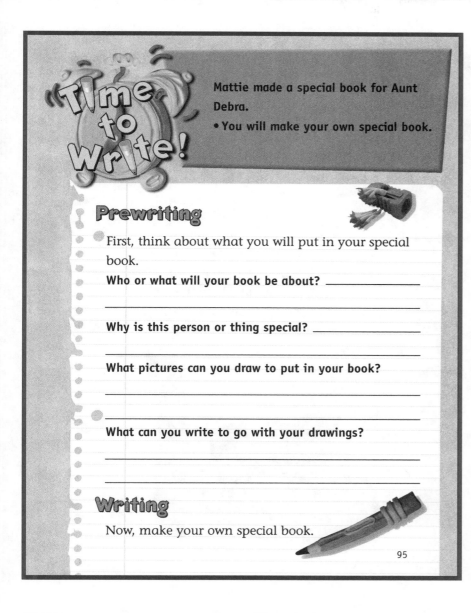

Time to Write!

Mattie made a special book for Aunt Debra.
• You will make your own special book.

Prewriting

First, think about what you will put in your special book.

Who or what will your book be about? _____

_____

Why is this person or thing special? _____

_____

What pictures can you draw to put in your book?

_____

_____

What can you write to go with your drawings?

_____

_____

Writing

Now, make your own special book.

95

Making Connections

Activity Links

- Have students tell the class about something that is special to them or to a family member, such as a musical instrument, a photo album, or a bicycle. Have students draw pictures of these special objects.
- Ask students to think about a special gift that they would like to receive. Have them give clues describing these special gifts and ask other students to guess what the gifts are.
- Have students make gifts for family members or friends. Encourage them to write short notes about how they made their gifts and include these with the gifts.

Reading Links

You may want to include these books in a discussion of special gifts and the joy of giving:
- *A Birthday Basket for Tia* by Pat Mora (Aladdin Picture Books, 1997).
- *Gifts Children Can Make: Creative Presents for Family and Friends* by Beth Murray (Boyds Mills Press, 1994).
- *Something Special for Me* by Vera B. Williams (William Morrow & Company, 1983).

Prewriting

Explain to students that writing answers to the questions will help them think about the book they will make.

Writing

Encourage students to be as creative as possible in decorating their books. Have them use brightly colored paper, pens, pencils, and crayons, and include drawings, photographs, or pictures they cut from magazines.

Sharing

Organize students into small groups and have them share their books with each other. Have students display their books in the classroom or in a case in a school hallway.

Thinking About...

What Happens First, Next, and Last

Recognizing Sequence

Readers must recognize sequence to understand what they read. Recognizing sequence is essential to comprehension and is one of the first steps to identifying the causes and effects of actions. The activities in this unit will help students apply the strategy of recognizing sequence, thereby helping them make better sense of what they read.

Thinking About

What Happens First, Next, and Last

Read the story below. As you read, think about what happens first, next, and last.

Aunt Dell makes animals out of wood. First, she cuts the wood to the right size. Next, she shapes the wood to look like an animal. Then, she makes the wood very smooth. Last, she paints the wood. Sometimes she lets me help her paint.

96

Introducing the Strategy

Directions are a good way of discussing sequence with your students. Bring in a set of directions for a game or a recipe. Read the directions aloud to the students. Then have students generate a list of what they would do first, next, and so on. If possible, have students follow the directions exactly. Explain to students that when they read the selections in this unit they should think about what happens first, what happens next, and what happens last in each selection.

Applying the Strategy

Ask students to follow along as you read the selection in the pupil book, or have a volunteer read it. Tell them to think about the order of the steps that Aunt Dell goes through in making wooden animals.

What order did Aunt Dell follow to make the wooden animals? Write 1, 2, or 3 in front of each sentence.

I wondered if she could paint the wood first.

_____ She shapes the wood.

_____ She cuts the wood.

_____ She paints the wood.

What is another step that Aunt Dell does?

_____

_____

_____

Read and Think

• Read the stories.
• Stop at each box. Answer the question.
• Think about what comes first, next, and last.

97

Read and Think

• Remind students that answering the questions in the boxes will help them think about the selections.
• Tell them that they can write as much or as little as they need to answer the questions.
• Encourage them to think about the sequence of events in the selections they read.

Discussing the Strategy

Have students complete the sequence questions independently or as a group. Ask students what they were thinking about while the selection was read. Ask questions such as the following:
• *What does Aunt Dell do first, next, and last?*
• *When is it important to do something in order?*
• *Have you ever forgotten one of the steps in following directions?*

Explain to students that they will be thinking about sequence, or what comes first, next, and last, as they read the selections in this unit.

How Many Stars in the Sky?

Strategy Focus

Recognizing the sequence of events in a selection.

Story at a Glance

A boy and his father drive to different places to count the stars in the night sky.

Vocabulary

You may want to introduce the following words to your students:

gazing   beamed
distance   basking
neon

Getting Students Started

• **Introducing the Selection**

Ask students if they have ever been curious about something in nature. For example, did they ever try to figure out why the sun is warm or what clouds are made of? Tell them that in this selection a young boy tries to find out how many stars are in the sky.

• **Purpose for Reading**

Students read to discover how the boy and his father try to count the stars in the sky.

How Many Stars in the Sky?

By Lenny Hort

 This story is about a boy who wants to count the stars. Read to find out how the boy and his father try to count the stars.

How many stars in the sky?

Mama was away that night and I couldn't sleep. Mama knows all about the sun and stars. But she was away and I didn't want to wake Daddy. So I stared out the window asking myself: how many stars in the sky?

98

I could count so many just from my room. I leaned out the window and I could count even more. That was just gazing over the backyard. How many stars in the sky?

 1 What do you think the boy will do next?

I went outside with a pad and pencil. I started to count. I filled up one whole page of the pad.

Strategy Tip

Tell students that a story is made up of many events. Every story has a beginning, a middle, and an end. Tell students that they will better understand what they are reading if they think about what happens first and try to predict what might happen next in a story.

Possible Responses
Question 1

. . . .

He is going to count stars.
This student makes a prediction supported by the selection. Ask, "How do you think he might do this?"

Maybe he will look in a book.
This student is using background knowledge to make a prediction about what might happen next. Ask, "Why do you think he might look in a book?"

go to sleep
This student has made an appropriate, but inaccurate, prediction about what might happen next. Ask, "What has the boy been doing so far in the story?"

But there were lots of stars hidden behind the trees. The house blocked out even more. The streetlamp was so bright I couldn't see stars anywhere near it. How many stars in the sky?

I climbed high up into my treehouse. I started at the Big Dipper and counted in a great circle all around the sky. I filled up page after page of the pad.

2 What makes the boy decide to climb up the tree?

But when I got back to the Dipper it wasn't where I remembered it. I must have been out so long that the stars had moved. Old ones had set. New ones had risen. How many stars in the sky?

★ 100

Possible Responses Question 2

He can see more stars.
Recognizing sequence is often the beginning of understanding cause and effect. This student understands the main reason the boy decided to climb the tree. Ask, "Why couldn't he count the stars from the ground?"

To be in his treehouse.
This student has stated a detail from the selection, but may not be understanding what motivated the boy to climb into his treehouse. Ask, "Why did he want to be in his treehouse? What could he see from there that he couldn't see from the ground?"

He still can't count them.
This student takes the question one step further and makes a prediction about what might happen after the boy climbs the tree. Ask, "What makes you think so?"

I climbed down from the treehouse and there was Daddy. "I couldn't sleep," I said.

"I can't sleep either," he said. "Your mama won't be back till tomorrow."

I told him how I wanted to count all the stars in the sky.

"If your mama was here," Daddy said, "I bet she'd know. Maybe you and I can find someplace where it'll be easier to count them."

101

My dog hopped in the truck with us and we drove into town. The streets were quiet, but lots of streetlights were burning. We could see the bright city skyline in the distance.

Daddy and I counted twenty-five or twenty-six stars. He said he thought one of them was the planet Jupiter. "This isn't a good place to see stars," I said.

102

"It's not a bad place to count them, though," he said. "But it's still too hard. Let's go where it'll be really easy."

We drove into the city. The big clock by the tunnel said 2:45, but neither one of us felt like sleeping.

We parked by Mama's office. There was a department store with brightly lit displays in every window. There were streetlamps on every corner.

103

There were dazzling neon signs. Headlights flashed from a steady stream of cars. Powerful searchlights beamed from the roofs of the skyscrapers.

And I couldn't see any stars at all. "I count exactly one," said Daddy. "No, wait," he said, "it's an airplane."

"Maybe the stars just don't want to be counted," I said.

We drove back through the tunnel. I was tired, and I thought we were going home. But instead, Daddy drove us deep into the country.

3   Why did Daddy drive to the country?

Possible Responses
Question 3

....

They were tired.
   In this section, the author does say that the boy was tired, but this response does not explain why the father would drive farther into the country. Ask, "The boy is tired, but are they going home now? Why did the father decide to leave the city and go into the country?"

To see stars.
   This student has very briefly summarized the basic event. Encourage the student to elaborate on his or her response by asking, "Where did they first try to see stars? Why did Daddy think the country would be a better place to see stars?"

It was hard to see with all the lights in the sky.
   This response indicates strong reading skills and a thorough comprehension of the sequence of events in the story.

There weren't any cars. There weren't any streetlights. There weren't any houses. Even the moon had set. And I knew we could never count all the stars.

No matter where I looked, new ones appeared every time I blinked my eyes. Daddy pointed up above and showed me the Milky Way. The stars were so thick I couldn't tell one from another.

We were much too tired to drive anymore, so we slept underneath the stars that night.

106

It was daylight when we woke. "Daddy,"
I said, "all those stars are always out there
even when we can't see them, right?"

"Of course they are," he said.

"Can we try to count them again some
time?" I asked.

"Any night you feel like it," he said, "you
and me and Mama can all go out together."

Supply students with dark-
colored construction paper
(dark brown, black, or blue)
and pastel chalks to make
their own night sky pictures.

After Reading

It is very important to have students read and discuss their responses to the questions in the boxes.

Discussing the Think-Alongs

- Give as many students as possible a chance to share what they wrote in one of the boxes.
- Have students review the sequence of events in the selection by asking the following questions:
  - *What does the boy in the selection do first?*
  - *What do the boy and his father do next?*
  - *How does the story end?*
- Ask students to tell what happened because the boy wanted to count the stars.

Reteaching

For those students who have not written or are having difficulty with the activity:

- Read the selection aloud to students who are having difficulty working on their own.
- Discuss the idea of sequence with students. Talk about sequence words such as "first," "then," "next," "so," and "at the end."
- Ask students to complete a sequence of events list that you start for them. Use the following model:
  - *First, the boy wanted to count the stars.*
  - *So, he _____.*
  - *His father first took the boy to _____.*
  - *They couldn't see stars there.*
  - *So, they next went to the _____.*

I could hardly wait to see Mama and tell her about it. In a little while we'd all be back home. But now I was glad just to be standing there with Daddy, basking in the warmth of the one star we could see—and that was the Sun.

 4 Did the boy get to do what he wanted during the night?

108

Possible Responses
Question 4

No, because he still didn't know how many stars there are.

He might try again when his mom helps.

Each of these responses demonstrates an understanding of the sequence of events in the reading. They also reflect the belief that the boy did not achieve everything he set out to do in the beginning of the story, but he may with help from his mother.

Yes, because he spent the night counting the stars.

In this response, the student has stated an opinion and demonstrated an understanding of the sequence of events in the story.

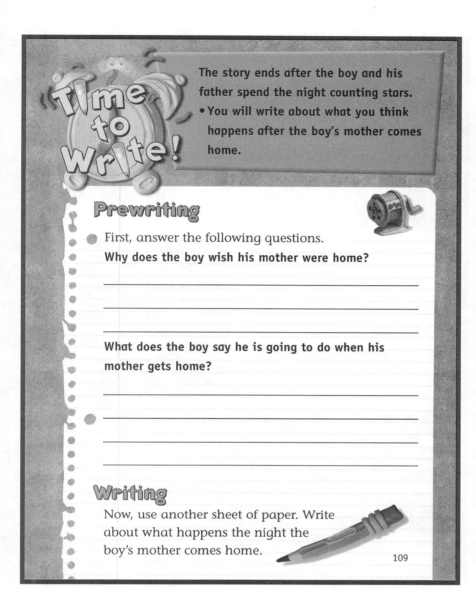

Time to Write!

The story ends after the boy and his father spend the night counting stars.
• You will write about what you think happens after the boy's mother comes home.

Prewriting

First, answer the following questions.

Why does the boy wish his mother were home?

_____

_____

_____

What does the boy say he is going to do when his mother gets home?

_____

_____

_____

_____

Writing

Now, use another sheet of paper. Write about what happens the night the boy's mother comes home.

109

Making Connections

Activity Links

- Have students write a description of the night sky that they can see from their rooms at night. Tell them to add details so that the reader can easily picture what they are describing.
- Put large sheets of paper over one wall of the classroom and have students paint a mural of the night sky.
- Take students to the library where they can read books about the stars and planets.
- The night that the boy spends with his father is a special night. Have students draw a picture and write about a special time they had with someone in their family.

Reading Links

You may want to include these books in a discussion about the night and stars:

- *Night on Neighborhood Street* by Eloise Greenfield (Penguin, 1991).
- *The Sky Is Full of Stars* by Franklyn Mansfield Branley (HarperTrophy, 1983).
- *The Big Dipper (A Let's-Read-and-Find-Out Book)* by Franklyn Mansfield Branley (HarperCollins Juvenile Books, 1991).

Prewriting

Explain to students that answering the questions will help them think about what they know about the boy's mother from the selection. This will help them think about what might happen after the boy's mother comes home. Tell them to think about what they are going to write about as they answer the questions.

Writing

Remind students that they need to think about what the order of events is in the selection, and what they picture might happen next.

Sharing

Have students read their stories to the class or to each other in small groups. Alternatively, have students act out their stories.

Strategy Focus

Recognizing the sequence of events in a selection.

Story at a Glance

This selection tells how beavers build their dams and lodges, which keep them safe from predators.

Vocabulary

You may want to introduce the following words to your students:

beaver   lodge
stumps   tunnel

Getting Students Started

• Introducing the Selection

Ask students to share what they already know about beavers and the houses they build. Ask them if they have ever seen a beaver dam. Ask them to describe beavers. Have students discuss why they think beavers cut down trees and build dams. Tell students that in this story they will read how beavers cut down trees, build dams, build their homes, and stay safe from larger animals.

• Purpose for Reading

Students read to learn about beavers and how they build their houses.

Beaver's Day

By Christine Butterworth

This story is about beavers. Beavers build dams and houses. Read the story to learn how the beavers build their houses.

It is a hot summer day. This beaver is hard at work. It is cutting down trees to make a dam. It bites the trees with sharp, yellow teeth.

Look at these tree stumps. The trees have been cut down by beavers.

110

The beaver works by a river. It needs the trees to make a dam across the river. It cuts the trees into short logs. It uses the logs to make a dam.

 1 What are you thinking about now?

Another beaver comes to help. It takes a log and swims to the dam. It fits the log into the wall of the dam.

The beavers push mud around the logs to keep them in place. They put sticks on the top of the dam. Soon the dam is as high as a tall person.

111

Strategy Tip

Tell students that this selection describes a sequence of events, one after the other. Tell them that thinking about what happens first and what happens next will help them think about why the events occur.

Possible Responses
Question 1

It would be hard to cut down a tree by just chewing on it. Beavers must have sharp teeth.
This student is thinking about a detail mentioned in the reading, and is repeating an important fact about beavers' teeth.

Why do beavers want to make dams?
Questions are often a sign that a student is following a logical thought sequence and trying to relate the sequence to causes and effects.

Encourage the student to answer his or her own question by asking, "Why do you think beavers make dams?"

I wonder how the beavers are so smart. They know all about building dams.
This response shows the student looking for information beyond what the text has provided. Ask, "How do you think beavers have learned to build dams?"

The beavers use the dam to make a lake. The water in the river is held back by the dam. Soon the water makes a deep lake behind the dam.

 2 How do the beavers build a dam?

Then the beavers can make their home. Their home is called a lodge.

Possible Responses
Question 2

They keep adding logs and the dam gets bigger and bigger.
In this response the student shows a general understanding of the beavers' dam building process. To encourage the student to focus on the sequential steps the beavers take to build their dams, ask, "What steps do the beavers follow to build a dam?"

They help each other and they pack mud between the logs. What is it for?
This student describes two important aspects of the dam building process, and asks an insightful question based on an understanding of this section. Ask, "What else do they do besides pack mud between the logs? Why do you think they are building the dam?"

They just keep adding logs and mud and then they have a lake.
This student states some of the steps the beavers take in building their dam. To clarify the sequence, ask, "What are they building when they add logs and mud?"

They cut down more trees to make the lodge. They make a pile of logs in the middle of the lake.

They make two tunnels deep under the water at the bottom of the pile of logs. The other ends of the tunnels come up inside the lodge. The beavers make a room where they can sleep inside the lodge.

 3 How do the beavers build their house?

113

Possible Responses Question 3

They cut down more logs and build tunnels under the logs.

This response demonstrates an understanding of some of the steps the beavers take in building their house. Ask, "What do they do after they cut down more logs, but before they dig tunnels?"

piles of logs and digging tunnels

Students may respond to questions in the boxes with single related words or phrases. Encourage this student to think about the steps the beavers take in building their house by asking, "What do the beavers do first to make their house? What do they do with the piles of logs? When do they dig tunnels?"

What's a lodge?

This student is questioning a vocabulary word in the reading. Encourage the student to define this word independently by using the story context. Then discuss the meaning of the word, telling the student that a lodge is a house.

The beavers are hungry after all their hard work. One beaver finds a stick and chews the bark. The other eats some water lily leaves.

This beaver is resting in the sun to dry its fur. Beavers' coats are thick and soft. But their tails have no fur. They are wide and flat. The beavers comb their fur with their claws.

They swim back to the lodge and sit on top of it. They do not see a bear on one side of the lake. The bear is looking for food.

A beaver in the water sees the bear. It smacks the water with its flat tail. Slap! The sound tells all the beavers that there is danger nearby.

4 How does a beaver warn other beavers about danger?

Possible Responses Question 4

They slap their tails on the water.

This student has accurately answered the question, which shows good reading comprehension and an understanding of story sequence. Ask, "What do you think will happen after the beaver slaps his tail on the water?"

The beaver makes a sound.

This response shows a basic understanding of the question and this section of the reading, but it could use elaboration. Ask, "How does the beaver make a sound?"

Did the beaver see the bear?

This student may not have understood the last paragraph in this section. Have the student re-read this paragraph, and then ask him or her to tell how a beaver warns other beavers about danger.

There is a mud slide down the side of the lodge. The beavers slide down it. Splash!
They dive deep under the water. They go into the lodge to hide from the bear.

116

Beavers can swim fast under water. They find the way into the lodge. The tunnel is deep under water. Other animals cannot get in. The beavers will be safe in the lodge.

5 What do you think will happen next?

117

Possible Responses
Question 5

The beavers will stay in their lodge. It is safe there.

In this response, the student has accurately predicted what will happen next based on a clear understanding of the sequence of events in the reading. Ask, "What might happen if the beavers leave the lodge?"

They got away from the bear!

While this response shows that the student has understood one event in the sequence of events that just occurred in the text, he or she has not predicted what will happen next. Say, "Yes, that's true. What do you think the beavers will do next? What do you think the bear will do next?"

The bear will try to break the beaver lodge.

This student is making a prediction based on what has happened in the reading and perhaps on background knowledge of bears. Ask, "What do you think the beavers will do if the bear breaks their lodge?"

After Reading

It is very important to have students read and discuss their responses to the questions in the boxes.

Discussing the Think-Alongs

- Give as many students as possible a chance to share what they wrote in one of the boxes.
- Ask students how thinking about what happens first, next, and last helps them understand the story.
- Ask students to tell why the beavers build their houses the way that they do. Ask what might happen to them if they do not build their houses so safely.

Reteaching

For those students who have not written or are having difficulty with the activity:

- Read the selection aloud to students who are having difficulty working on their own.
- Model your own thoughts about sequencing by discussing the order of events in the selection as you read it aloud to students.
- Ask students to review the sequence of the selection by asking questions such as the following:
  - *What did the beavers do first?*
  - *How did the beavers build the dam?*
  - *What did the beavers do after they built the dam?*
  - *How did the beavers escape from the bear?*

The bear looks at the beavers' lodge in the middle of the lake. It can smell the beavers, but it cannot get into the lodge. The bear goes away. The beavers are safe inside the lodge.

118

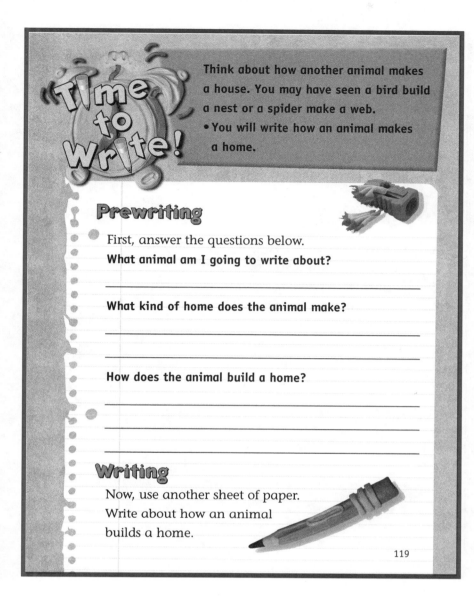

Time to Write!

Think about how another animal makes a house. You may have seen a bird build a nest or a spider make a web.

• You will write how an animal makes a home.

Prewriting

First, answer the questions below.

What animal am I going to write about?

_____

What kind of home does the animal make?

_____

_____

How does the animal build a home?

_____

_____

_____

Writing

Now, use another sheet of paper. Write about how an animal builds a home.

119

Prewriting

Explain to students that answering the questions will help them think about what they want to write about how an animal builds a home.

Writing

Remind students that they need to think about one animal and how that animal builds a home. They should tell what the home is like and the steps the animal takes to build it. If they can, they should tell why the animal builds the home in the way that it does. Possible animals include birds, squirrels, and rabbits.

Sharing

When students have finished, ask student volunteers to read their short description to the class. Encourage other students to ask questions about how the animal house is built.

Making Connections

Activity Links

• Have students create displays using the descriptions they wrote for the writing activity. Ask them to make or draw examples of these animal homes, or find pictures of these homes in books or magazines to create collages or a bulletin board display.

• Have students draw a picture of a beaver dam, a beaver lodge, and the tunnels the beavers use to get into and out of their lodge.

• Ask students to use an encyclopedia to learn more about beavers and whether beavers could live near the students' homes or school.

Reading Links

You may want to include these books in a discussion about beavers, mammals, and where animals live:

• *Beaver* by Glen Rounds (Holiday House, 1999).

• *Beavers Beware* by Barbara Brenner (Bantam, Bank Street, 1992).

• *About Mammals: A Guide for Children* by Cathryn P. Sill (Peachtree Publishers, 1997).

• *Armadillos Sleep in Dugouts; and Other Places Animals Live* by Pam Munoz Ryan (Hyperion Books, 1997).

How Spiders Got Eight Legs

Strategy Focus

Recognizing the sequence of events in a selection.

Story at a Glance

This selection tells a fictional story about how spiders got eight legs. The spider in this folktale goes through many different sets of animal legs before he ends up with eight spider legs.

Vocabulary

You may want to introduce the following words to your students:

spiders	*wishes*
jungle	*promise*
grant	*honestly*

Getting Students Started

• Introducing the Selection

Ask students if they have ever been curious about something in nature. For example, did they ever wonder why different animals look the way they do? Did they ever wonder why zebras have stripes or giraffes have long necks? Tell students that this story explains why one animal, the spider, has eight legs.

• Purpose for Reading

Students read to learn one story that explains how spiders got eight legs.

Retold by Katherine Mead

Let's Read

This folktale tells how spiders got eight legs. Read to find out why spiders have so many legs.

Long ago in Africa, spiders had only two legs. There was one spider who was very selfish. He wanted to be better than all the other animals in the jungle. But he did not like to work hard.

Every year, there was a big race in the jungle. All the animals wanted to win. They practiced running every day.

120

Spider thought, "I am much better than the others. I'll think of a way to win this year's race without working hard."

1 What does Spider want to happen?

Spider watched all the animals run. He thought that Ostrich, Giraffe, or Cheetah could win the race. Spider could not run as fast as any of them. But he did not worry. He had a plan.

121

Possible Responses
Question 1

He wants to win the race.
This student's response is supported by the selection, but it could use elaboration. Ask, "How do you think he will try to win the race? Do you think he will practice like the other animals?"

He wants to win but does not want to work.
This student provides a response that is supported by the text. This response also shows an understanding of the spider's motivation and the series of events presented in the story up to this point.

He wants to have eight legs.
This student is responding to the title of the selection rather than to this section of the reading. Encourage the student to respond to the first two paragraphs by asking, "Why do you think he wants to have eight legs?"

Spider thought, "Ostrich has such strong legs. If I had legs like his, I could win the race." Spider went to the river to see Great Hippo, the hippopotamus. He was the wisest animal. He could grant wishes.

Spider called out, "Great Hippo, I wish to have strong legs like Ostrich."

"Why do you wish to have legs like Ostrich?" Great Hippo asked.

"I have to win the race!" said Spider.

Great Hippo said, "I will give you strong legs, but you must promise me something. One day, I will ask you a question. You must answer honestly."

Spider said, "That will be easy." So his wish was granted.

122

Spider tried to run on his new legs, but it was too hard. He asked Ostrich for help.

Ostrich said, "Watch, my friend. I'll show you how to run with those legs."

Spider watched, but still he could not run.

Spider was mad. He went back to see Great Hippo. He said, "I cannot run with these legs. I wish to have four long legs like Giraffe."

Great Hippo asked, "Why do you wish to have legs like Giraffe?"

Spider said, "I want to take long steps like Giraffe. I have to win the race!"

 2 What are you thinking about now?

Possible Responses
Question 2

He will not be able to run with them.

This student has already recognized the pattern in the selection that guides the sequence of events. Ask, "What makes you think so?"

He will win the race because he will run fast.

Although this response is not an accurate prediction, this is a reasonable prediction to make based on the information presented in the reading so far. Ask, "Do you think spider will have any trouble with giraffe legs?"

Maybe he will visit Giraffe next.

This student focuses on another pattern in the selection to make a prediction—the Spider's visits to other animals. Ask, "Why do you think he will visit Giraffe next?"

Great Hippo said, "I will give you four long legs, but you must promise me something. One day, I will ask you a question. You must answer honestly."

Spider said, "That will be easy." So his wish was granted.

Spider tried to run on his long legs, but it was too hard. He asked Giraffe for help.

Giraffe said, "Watch, my friend. I'll show you how to run with those legs."

Spider watched, but still he could not run.

125

Organize students into pairs. Have students in each pair take turns retelling the story of "How Spiders Got Eight Legs." Students can use the pictures from the book to help them in their retelling.

Spider was really mad. He went back to see Great Hippo. He said, "I cannot run on these long legs. I wish for eight legs."

Great Hippo asked, "Why do you wish for eight legs?"

Spider said, "Cheetah is the fastest four-legged animal. I could run twice as fast as Cheetah if I had eight legs."

 3 Why does Spider want eight legs?

Possible Responses
Question 3

He wants to run fast.

He wants to win the race.
Both of these responses are supported by what Spider says in the selection and reflect an understanding of the cause-and-effect relationship in the reading. Ask, "Do you think he will be able to run fast and win the race with eight legs?"

Don't know. It will be too hard to run.
This response reflects a critical reading of the selection. The student is questioning Spider's desire for eight legs, and understands the pattern established in the story in which Spider cannot learn to run with any of the legs he receives.

Great Hippo said, "I will give you eight legs, but you must promise me something. One day, I will ask you a question. You must answer honestly."

Spider said, "That will be easy." So his wish was granted.

4 What do you think will happen next?

127

Possible Responses
Question 4

Spider won't be able to run with the legs.

This is a reasonable prediction based on an understanding of the sequence of events and the pattern established in the story. Ask, "Why don't you think Spider will be able to run with these new legs? Do you think it will be easy for Spider to tell the truth when he is later asked a question?"

Spider will not be honest. He will lie to get the legs.

This student is making a prediction based on an insightful understanding of Spider's character and motivations. Ask, "Why do you think Spider will lie? Why does Spider want the legs so badly?"

Spider will win the race.

This is a logical prediction based on the reading so far. Ask, "Why do you think Spider will win? Do you think that Spider might have trouble winning because of the way he is trying to win? Do you think that being honest will be easy for Spider?"

Spider tried to run with eight legs, but it was too hard. He asked Cheetah for help.

Cheetah said, "I don't know how to run with eight legs. I could only show you if you had four legs like me."

Spider was madder than ever. He went back to see Great Hippo again. He yelled, "These eight legs don't work! How am I going to win the race?"

Great Hippo did not answer. He just walked into the river to swim.

Spider made his way home. He was still angry. He sat down and thought very hard. How could he win the race with eight legs? Suddenly, he had an idea! He laughed and went to sleep.

On the day of the race, Cheetah could hear someone yelling for help. He said, "That sounds like Spider. I'll go check on him."

Cheetah ran off to Spider's house. Spider was lying down and crying out with pain.

> **5** What are you thinking about now?

Possible Responses
Question 5

He will fool Cheetah.
This response demonstrates good comprehension of the sequence of events, and makes an insightful prediction. Ask, "What made you think that Spider might try to fool Cheetah?"

Why did he laugh?
This student is responding to an event in the story that indicates Spider's plan to trick Cheetah. Encourage the student to try to answer his or her own question. Then ask, "What do you think Spider might do next? Why might this make him laugh?"

His new legs might hurt.
Although this is not an accurate prediction, this is a reasonable assumption for the student to make. Say, "You are right that his new legs might hurt, but keep reading to see if you think that is what is bothering him."

"Spider, what's wrong?" Cheetah asked.

Spider said, "I am very sick. Take me to see Great Hippo. He'll know what to do."

Cheetah said, "Great Hippo is waiting at the finish line. I will take you to him."

Spider climbed on Cheetah's back. Cheetah began to run as fast as he could. The race had already started. Cheetah was behind all the animals. Spider cried louder with pain. Then Cheetah ran faster.

130

Cheetah ran past the slowest animals. He ran past faster animals. Then Cheetah ran past Ostrich. He ran past Giraffe. Cheetah ran faster and faster until he took the lead.

Spider could see the finish line. He climbed onto the tip of Cheetah's nose. Everyone cheered as Cheetah crossed the finish line. Great Hippo announced, "Cheetah's the winner!"

Spider yelled, "Wait! Cheetah didn't win. I DID! I crossed the finish line first. I won by a nose!"

131

After Reading

It is very important to have students read and discuss their responses to the questions in the boxes.

Discussing the Think-Alongs

- Give as many students as possible a chance to share what they wrote in one of the boxes.
- Have students explain what they were thinking when they wrote.
- Ask students how paying attention to the sequence of events helps them better understand the selection.

Reteaching

For those students who have not written or are having difficulty with the activity:

- Read the selection aloud to students who are having difficulty working on their own.
- Make a set of index cards listing the main events in the selection. Mix up the cards and have students sort them into the correct sequence. Next, read each of these index cards aloud and have a different student tell about the scene in his or her own words.
- Ask students to review the sequence of events in the selection by asking the following questions:
    - *What did the spider want to do?*
    - *How did he think he might do this?*
    - *What finally happened to the spider?*

Great Hippo looked at Spider. He said, "I have a question. Remember that you promised to answer it honestly. Who REALLY won the race?"

Spider was worried. He knew he had to be honest. He said, "I tried to trick all of you. Cheetah is the real winner."

 6 Why did Spider have to be honest?

Great Hippo smiled. He said, "Thank you for being honest. Now I will make those eight legs work just right for you."

From then on, spiders everywhere have had eight legs. And they work just right.

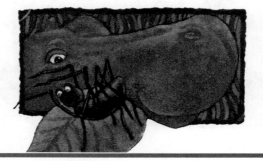

132

Possible Responses
Question 6

He promised the Hippo.

He wasn't being fair to Cheetah.

He knew he didn't really run the race.

All of these responses demonstrate comprehension of the story's sequence of events, and the ethical dilemma involved with spider's desire to win.

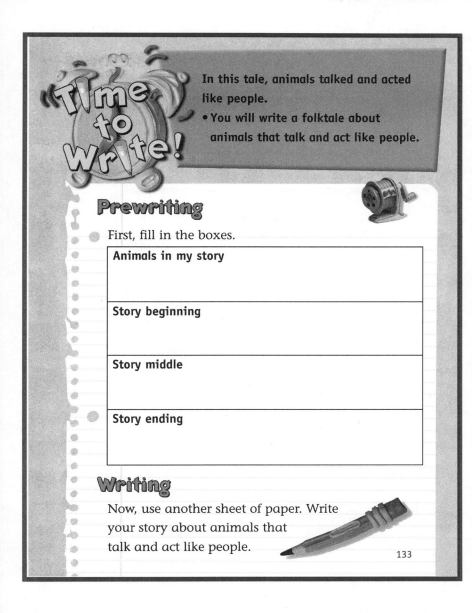

Time to Write!

In this tale, animals talked and acted like people.

• You will write a folktale about animals that talk and act like people.

Prewriting

First, fill in the boxes.

Animals in my story
Story beginning
Story middle
Story ending

Writing

Now, use another sheet of paper. Write your story about animals that talk and act like people.

133

Making Connections

Activity Links

- Have students make their own spiders using egg cartons and pipe cleaners. Have a book of spider pictures available so that students can use paint, crayons, or pens to make realistic markings on their spiders.
- Ask students to observe a spider that they see at home or outside. Have the students report to the class about what they observed the spider doing.
- Help students make their own spider webs. To make a web, glue or attach two thin sticks at right angles (in the shape of an *X*). Then, secure the *X* with a long piece of yarn, and continue looping colorful yarn around the sticks.

Reading Links

You may want to include these books in a discussion about folktales and spiders:

- *The Adventures of Spider: West African Folktales* by Jerry Pinkney (Little, Brown and Co., 1992).
- *Mighty Spiders!* by Fay Robinson (Cartwheel Books, 1996).
- *Coyote Places the Stars* by Harriet P. Taylor (Simon & Schuster, 1993).

Prewriting

Explain to students that answering the questions will help them think about what they want to write about in their folktales. Remind them that they can write about family pets, farm animals, or animals in the wild. The only requirement for their folktales is that they write about animal characters who talk and act like people.

Writing

Remind students that they should think about who will read their stories. Encourage students to make sure that their stories are interesting and easy to follow so that their classmates, teacher, or parents can read them.

Sharing

When students have finished writing their stories, have them draw accompanying illustrations. Help students compile their stories into a bound book. Ask students to share their individual stories with the class, and display their books in the class or in a case in a school hallway.

The Tests

The next three selections are like standardized-test reading comprehension passages, with questions at the end of each selection. However, boxes with think-along questions appear within the selections to allow students to practice their think-along strategies.

Note that these selections are not designed to test specific reading strategies, but rather are designed to show students how thinking along will help them comprehend what they are reading and better answer questions about what they have read.

Introducing the Tests to Students

Remind students that this section is like the one that they completed earlier in the book. Tell them to apply the think-along process as they read the selections and then answer the questions at the end of each selection.

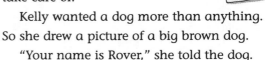
Thinking Along on Tests

- Read each story.
- Stop at each box. Answer the question.
- Answer the questions at the end of each story.

What happened to Kelly's dog?

"I wish, I wish!" Kelly said.

"I wish that I could have a dog."

"No dogs," Mother said.

"We can't keep a dog here. A dog would be too hard to take care of."

Kelly wanted a dog more than anything. So she drew a picture of a big brown dog.

"Your name is Rover," she told the dog.

> 1 What are you thinking about now?

134

Possible Responses

Question 1

A picture is not a dog!
This student demonstrates a literal understanding of the reading, and is either questioning or criticizing the likelihood of the events in the reading. Ask, "How might drawing a picture help Kelly imagine that she has a dog?"

Why won't the mom let her get a dog?
This student is empathizing with the main character and is questioning the mother's decision, which shows strong reading comprehension and

critical thinking skills. Encourage the student to think of reasons why Kelly's mother might not let her have a dog.

I would make my dog black and white and call him Speckles.
This student has made a personal connection with the reading by imagining what he or she would draw if in the same situation as Kelly.

Kelly went to sleep with the picture of Rover by her side. She was very happy. But then when she looked at the paper, her dog was gone!

Outside, a man was shaking his rake. "A big brown dog ran through my garden," he said. "Do you own that dog?" the man asked.

"Not me," Kelly said. "We can't keep a dog where I live."

Then Kelly woke up. The picture of Rover was gone. The wind had blown it under her bed. Kelly didn't see it there. "A dog really would be too hard to take care of," she thought.

---

2 What are you thinking about now?

135

The Selections and Questions

The three selections in this test section are of different types: two fictional stories and one poem. Each is followed by four multiple-choice questions and one short-answer question. The question format is typical of many standardized and criterion-referenced tests. The purpose-setting question format at the beginning of each selection is similar to that used on many nationally standardized tests. These questions help students to focus on a purpose for reading.

Possible Responses
Question 2

She should have drawn a nice little dog that would be good. This student has created a thoughtful solution to Kelly's problem. Discuss different ways that one can create imaginary characters and enjoy them. Ask, "How might the story have ended if she had drawn a nice little dog?"

I think she should find Rover and take him home! In this response, the student is either continuing to think about what Kelly could do with her imaginary dog, or the student may be confused about whether or not the dog is real. To clarify, ask, "Where should she look for Rover?"

Oh, just a dream! I guess she didn't really wake up before, and now she has. This response reflects the student's understanding of a key aspect of this story. Ask, "What is different when Kelly wakes up in her dream and when she really wakes up later?"

Darken the circle for the correct answer.

**1. Kelly gets a dog by
_____.**

Ⓐ opening her window

Ⓑ asking a man for it

Ⓒ chasing and catching it

Ⓓ drawing it on paper

**2. Outside, Rover is busy
_____.**

Ⓐ making a new friend

Ⓑ getting in trouble

Ⓒ chasing cars

Ⓓ trying to find Kelly

**3. We can tell from this story
that Kelly was _____.**

Ⓐ hiding from her dog

Ⓑ cleaning her room

Ⓒ having a dream

Ⓓ talking to her mother

**4. Where is Rover at the end
of the story?**

Ⓐ on the picture under the
bed

Ⓑ chasing a cat up a tree

Ⓒ playing in a man's garden

Ⓓ jumping through the
window

Write your answer on the lines below.

5. Why didn't Kelly tell the man that the dog was hers?

_____

_____

_____

Answers and Analysis

1. D; evaluative/critical
2. B; inferential
3. C; inferential
4. A; literal
5. Evaluative/critical.

Answers may include any of the following points:

- Kelly was embarrassed.
- She didn't want to be blamed for drawing the dog.
- Kelly doubted that a picture of a dog could really do those things, or that a pretend dog could turn into a real dog.

Scoring Question 5:

2 = An answer that includes one or more of the points listed above, or another reasonable motivation.

0 = An answer that does not state a possible motivation for Kelly's behavior.

Explanation of Comprehension Skills

Literal: The answer is specifically stated in the text.

Inferential: The answer can be inferred from the text, but it is not specifically stated.

Evaluative/Critical: The answer is based on an evaluation of the text.

Who is Munchie?

Mother ran up and down the hall.
She was swinging a big straw broom!
She stopped to look in every room,
And Pete could hear her call:
"There's a mouse!
There's a mouse!"
She had spotted poor Munchie
in a minute.
"I won't have a house with a
mouse living in it!
"There's a mouse!
There's a mouse!
There's a mouse in this house!"

| **1** | What are you thinking about now? |

137

Possible Responses
Question 1

Munchie is a mouse! I don't blame her.

In this response, the student appears to empathize with Mother and understands her distress that there is a mouse in the house. To clarify, ask, "What don't you blame her for?"

What's wrong with a little mouse? All that yelling.

This student challenges Mother's behavior, and questions whether the mouse should cause such alarm.

Ask, "What would you do if you found a mouse in your house?"

My mom used a broom to try to sweep mice.

This student has connected personal experience to the reading. Ask, "What did you think when your mother used a broom to sweep the mice away?"

Munchie ran fast—right past Pete.

He ran down the hall, and then

He ran outside as Dad came in.

He ran away fast on tiny feet.

"Oh, please let Munchie go!" Pete cried.

"He's my friend! I like to watch him play.

He's sure to come back in today.

He doesn't like to play outside."

Mother said, "Then I don't mind at all!

Does he have a horn that he can play?

If he does, then he can stay."

Pete smiled and said, "As I recall,

He plays a piano that's very small."

 2 What are you thinking about now?

Possible Responses
Question 2

A horn and a piano? What kind of mouse is that?

This student seems surprised and confused by the joke at the end of the poem. To clarify, ask, "What about the horn and the piano? Who is supposed to play them? Do you think Mother and Pete really think that Munchie can play musical instruments?

I know where there's a mouse living. Never saw him play though.

In this response, the student relates the story to personal experience, and even continues with the poem's joke that mice can play musical instruments. Ask, "Do you think mice can really play musical instruments? Where does that mouse live?"

I can just see Dad's surprise.

This student is making a prediction by visualizing how Pete's father might react if he saw a mouse invited to stay because it might play music.

Darken the circle for the correct answer.

6. Munchie is a _____.

   Ⓐ brother

   Ⓑ mouse

   Ⓒ neighbor

   Ⓓ toy

7. Mother is upset because _____.

   Ⓐ Pete is playing outside

   Ⓑ Father is not home

   Ⓒ Munchie is in the house

   Ⓓ Pete is making fun of her

8. In this story, the word *play* means to have fun and to _____.

   Ⓐ make music

   Ⓑ pretend to be angry

   Ⓒ act very silly

   Ⓓ yell loudly

9. When Pete talks about the piano, he is _____.

   Ⓐ joking

   Ⓑ begging

   Ⓒ bragging

   Ⓓ crying

Write your answer on the lines below.

10. How do you think Munchie feels during this story?

_____

_____

_____

_____

139

Answers and Analysis

6. B; literal
7. C; inferential
8. A; inferential
9. A; evaluative/critical
10. Evaluative/critical.
Answers may include one or more reasonable assumptions, such as the following:

- He is afraid of Mother and her broom.
- He feels hurt and mad about having to go outside.
- He knows he will miss Pete when he is outside.
- He's a mouse, and he probably doesn't feel much.
- He is always hungry.

Scoring Question 10:

2 = Any reasonable assumption about how Munchie might feel.

0 = Response that does not reflect the perspective of the mouse.

Explanation of Comprehension Skills

Literal: The answer is specifically stated in the text.

Inferential: The answer can be inferred from the text, but it is not specifically stated.

Evaluative/Critical: The answer is based on an evaluation of the text.

Where does Nina go sailing?

The little sailboat sat on Grandpa's desk. It had two pointed sails tied to a center pole. Grandpa said that the pole was called a mast. The sails were white. The boat was a shiny dark blue. The name "Matilda" was painted on each side in tiny white letters.

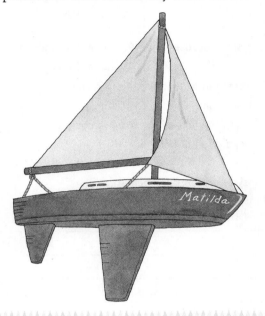

Nina would sit in the big chair in front of the desk. Grandpa thought Nina was watching him work. But Nina was staring at the sailboat. She would stare until everything around the boat was blurry. She thought the boat was out on a windy sea, and the sails were fat with wind. Nina was on the boat racing across the water. She was captain of the "Matilda."

> **1** What are you thinking about now?

Finally, one day, Grandpa asked her, "Would you like to have the sailboat?"
"Oh, yes," Nina said.

Possible Responses
Question 1

I can do that too when I look at something.

This response shows a personal connection and an ability to visualize what Nina is doing—staring and trying to imagine something. Ask, "What kinds of things do you look at and imagine?"

I don't get it! What is she doing?

This reader generates a question that shows he or she needs some help understanding the main idea of this story. Ask, "What do you think she is doing? Have you ever imagined doing something like sailing, running, or skiing? Have you ever tried to picture something imaginary by staring and letting your eyes go out of focus?"

Fat with wind! That's funny!

This student focuses on one of the details in the story and responds to the figurative language used in the selection. Ask, "What do you think it means if the sails are fat with wind?"

That day Nina stopped at a pond and put the sailboat into the water. But it would only move a little bit. She tapped it, but it only moved a little bit more. A light wind blew, but the sails did not move. Nina leaned back in the grass and stared. But it was not the same.

The next afternoon Grandpa came into his office and found Nina in the big chair. The little sailboat was on his desk. He did not ask Nina why she had brought it back. He could see Nina staring at the boat. Nina was out to sea again.

 2   What are you thinking about now?

Possible Responses
Question 2

Grandpa is happy. He gave Nina the boat. Then, he didn't have the boat or Nina. Now Nina and the boat are back.

This response shows an understanding of the sequence of events in the story. The student also uses this understanding to infer how Grandpa might feel about what has happened with Nina and the boat.

Maybe he will take her on a real sailboat.

This response makes a prediction that goes beyond the events in the story. Ask, "What makes you think this might happen?"

Why does he have this boat anyhow?

This student questions the usefulness of a model boat, looking for information about the characters beyond what the story provides. Encourage the student to answer his or her question by asking, "How could he use the boat?"

Darken the circle for the correct answer.

11. Where is the sailboat at the end of the story?

Ⓐ in a pond

Ⓑ on a chair

Ⓒ on Grandpa's desk

Ⓓ in the grass by the pond

13. What happened at the pond?

Ⓐ The wind blew the boat.

Ⓑ The boat sank.

Ⓒ The boat only moved a little.

Ⓓ The girl fell asleep.

12. What is the name of the sailboat?

Ⓐ Nina

Ⓑ Grandpa

Ⓒ Windy

Ⓓ Matilda

14. In this story, a mast is a _____.

Ⓐ kind of a desk

Ⓑ pole on a sailboat

Ⓒ special chair

Ⓓ strong wind

Write your answer on the lines below.

15. Why did Nina bring back the sailboat?

_____

_____

_____

_____

Making Connections

Discussion

After the students have completed the questions for all three selections, discuss with them what they wrote in the boxes. Ask students to tell what they wrote in a box and to explain why they wrote what they did. Then, have students discuss how writing in the boxes helped them to remember what the selection was about so they could better answer the questions at the end of the selections.

For your own curricular planning, you might also want to review what students have written in the boxes. Reading what students have written will give you an idea of how well they are comprehending what they read and whether they need additional review of the process of thinking along as they read.

Scoring

Refer to the discussion of test taking on page T11 of the teacher's edition for information on scoring and interpreting student scores.

Answers and Analysis

11. C; literal
12. D; literal
13. C; literal
14. B; literal
15. Evaluative/critical

Answers should focus on reasonable motivations Nina might have had for bringing the boat back, such as the following:

• The boat would not sail at the pond.

• The girl was happier dreaming about sailing the boat when it was on the desk than when she was trying to make it sail.

Scoring Question 15:

2 = Responses that indicate a reasonable explanation telling why Nina brought the boat back.

0 = Responses that do not offer reasonable explanations.

Explanation of Comprehension Skills

Literal: The answer is specifically stated in the text.

Inferential: The answer can be inferred from the text, but it is not specifically stated.

Evaluative/Critical: The answer is based on an evaluation of the text.

Acknowledgments

Grateful acknowledgment is made to the following authors and publishers for the use of copyrighted materials. Every effort has been made to obtain permission to use previously published material. Any errors or omissions are unintentional.

Beaver's Day by Christine Butterworth. Copyright © 1990 by Steck-Vaughn Company. Reprinted by arrangement with Macmillan Press Ltd.

"A Big Brother Knows . . . What a Little Brother Needs" by Vashanti Rahaman. Copyright © 1995 by Highlights for Children, Inc., Columbus, Ohio. Reprinted by permission of Highlights for Children, Inc.

The Case of the Missing Lunch by Jean Groce. From SIGNATURES, Grade 2, "The Case of the Missing Lunch," copyright © 1999 by Harcourt, Inc., reprinted by permission of the publisher.

The Doorbell Rang by Pat Hutchins. Copyright © 1986 by Pat Hutchins. By permission of Greenwillow Books, a division of William Morrow and Company, Inc.

A Gift to Share by Barbara Swett Burt. Copyright © 1998 by Steck-Vaughn Company.

How Many Stars in the Sky? by Lenny Hort. Text copyright © 1991 by Lenny Hort. Illustrations copyright © 1991 by James Ransome. By permission of Tambourine Books, a division of William Morrow and Company, Inc.

How Spiders Got Eight Legs retold by Katherine Mead. Copyright © 1998 by Steck-Vaughn Company.

It Happens to Everyone by Bernice Myers. Copyright © 1990 by Bernice Myers. By permission of Lothrop, Lee and Shepard Books, a division of William Morrow and Company, Inc.

"Jessie's Big Idea" by Carolyn Short. Copyright © 1997 by Highlights for Children, Inc., Columbus, Ohio. Reprinted by permission of Highlights for Children, Inc.

The Statue of Liberty by Lucille Recht Penner. Text copyright © 1995 by Lucille Recht Penner. Illustrations copyright © 1995 by Jada Rowland. Reprinted by arrangement with Random House, Inc.

"The Thinking Place" by Katie U. Vandergriff. Copyright © 1996 by Highlights for Children, Inc., Columbus, Ohio. Reprinted by permission of Highlights for Children, Inc.

When Winter Comes by Pearl Neuman. Copyright © 1989 by American Teacher Publications. Reprinted by permission of the publisher.

Illustration Credits

Steve Henry, pp. T16–28; Ken Bowser, pp. 4, 30, 66, 96; Bernice Myers, pp. 6–12; Pat Hutchins, pp. 14–20; Randy Verougstraete, pp. 22–28; Pamela Johnson, pp. 32–38; Jada Rowland, pp. 40–46; John Courtney, pp. 48–54; Ellen Joy Sasaki, pp. 56, 57, 59, 60, 62, 64, 134, 135, 137, 138, 140, 142; Jeff LeVan, pp. 68–74; Richard Roe, pp. 76–84; Béatrice Lebreton, pp. 86–94; James E. Ransome, pp. 98–108; Carol O'Malia, pp. 120–132.

Photography Credits

Cover (front) Sam Dudgeon; cover (back) © Steven Raymer; p. T4 © Jeff Dunn/Stock Boston; p. T5 © Steven Raymer; p. T8a Cindi Ellis; p. T8b Ian Shaw/Tony Stone Images; pp. T12–T15, 5, 31, 67, 97 Rick Williams; p. 110a ©Don Skillman/Animals Animals; p. 110b ©Gary R. Zahm/Bruce Coleman, Inc.; p. 111 ©Leonard Lee Rue III/Animals Animals; p. 112 CORBIS/Richard Hamilton Smith; p. 113 ©Perry D. Slocum/Animals Animals; p. 114a ©Johnny Johnson/Animals Animals; p. 114b ©Leonard Lee Rue III/Animals Animals; p. 115a ©Jonathan T. Wright/Bruce Coleman, Inc.; p. 115b ©Ted Levin/Animals Animals; p. 116 CORBIS/W. Perry Conway; p. 117 ©J.D. Taylor/Bruce Coleman, Inc.; p. 118 CORBIS/W. Perry Conway.